Foxhall Alexander Parker

The battle of Mobile Bay

and the capture of forts Powell, Gaines and Morgan, by the combined sea

and land forces of the United States

Foxhall Alexander Parker

The battle of Mobile Bay
and the capture of forts Powell, Gaines and Morgan, by the combined sea and land forces of the United States

ISBN/EAN: 9783337695736

Printed in Europe, USA, Canada, Australia, Japan

Cover: Foto ©ninafisch / pixelio.de

More available books at **www.hansebooks.com**

THE
BATTLE OF MOBILE BAY,

AND THE CAPTURE OF

FORTS POWELL, GAINES AND MORGAN,
BY THE
COMBINED SEA AND LAND FORCES OF THE UNITED STATES,
UNDER THE COMMAND OF
REAR-ADMIRAL DAVID GLASGOW FARRAGUT, AND
MAJOR-GENERAL GORDON GRANGER,
AUGUST, 1864.

BY

COMMODORE FOXHALL A. PARKER, U.S.N.,
AUTHOR OF "THE FLEETS OF THE WORLD," "FLEET TACTICS
UNDER STEAM," "SQUADRON TACTICS,"
ETC., ETC.

ACCOMPANIED BY TWO CHARTS,

PRINTED IN COLORS.

BOSTON:
A. WILLIAMS & CO.,
283 WASHINGTON STREET.
1878.

TO THE

OFFICERS, SEAMEN AND MARINES,

WHO SERVED UNDER FARRAGUT,
DURING THE MONTH OF AUGUST, 1864,

This Volume is Dedicated.

PREFACE.

REGARDING the reputation for intrepidity gained by Federal and Confederate sailors and soldiers during our civil war as the common heritage of the American people, I determined, last year, at the instance of The Military Historical Society of Massachusetts, to write the story of Mobile Bay: This, when completed, I read before the Society, (December 10th, 1877,) and the favorable reception it met with has induced me to give it to the public, the more especially as it is accompanied with a number of official reports, never before published, which cannot fail to interest the general reader and be of value to the historian.

As regards my own work, while I can truly say I have spared no pains myself to insure its correctness and completeness, I have to acknowledge my indebtedness to hosts of friends for their hearty co-operation in my task; and my especial thanks are due to Major-General Dabney H. Maury, of the late Confederate army, and to Professor A. D. Wharton, Principal of the Fogg School, at Nashville, Tennessee.

F. A. P.

U. S. NAVY YARD, BOSTON, MASS.,
      April 8, 1878.

THE
BATTLE OF MOBILE BAY,

AND

CAPTURE OF FORTS MORGAN, GAINES, AND POWELL.

THAT arm of the Gulf of Mexico, which, extending for thirty-five miles into the state of Alabama, and varying in width from seven to fifteen miles, is known as Mobile Bay, will ever be regarded with interest by the student of history; for there is scarcely a rood of its shores but has served as the last resting-place of one of the early discoverers, while the bay itself derives its name from the Indian town of Mauvila,[1] whose governor, the gigantic Tascaluça, received Hernando de Soto, seated,[2] while all around him stood, and his standard-bearer unfolded that banner which excited the astonishment of the Spaniards, and was so soon to be waved defiantly in their midst: for in Mauvila's blood-stained streets it was that, among other cavaliers of note, De Soto's two nephews fell.[3]

During the seventeenth and eighteenth centuries, Mobile Bay fell into the hands of the French and Spaniards, alternately; in 1812, it was taken possession of by United States troops and annexed to Mississippi territory, and, in

1819, it became included within the limits of the state of Alabama.

On the 15th of September, 1814, the stillness that usually hangs over its sluggish waters was for the first time broken by the roar of heavy artillery, (for it was on that day that the British squadron, under Percy, was repulsed in its attack on the little redoubt called Fort Bowyer, with a loss of one vessel, the Hermes, and over two hundred men;) and, on August 5, 1864, it was rudely awakened from its half-century slumber by the noise of the great battle which it has become my province to describe.

Alabama, having thrown her sword into the scale of the Southern Confederacy in January, 1861, turned her first thoughts toward the security of her only seaport, Mobile. To this end, Governor Moore seized upon the United States arsenal in the city, and garrisoned, with state troops, forts Morgan and Gaines.[4] As these forts, being at the entrance of Mobile Bay, were the keys to Mobile from the gulf side, a brief description of their condition and armament must now be given. Fort Morgan, on the site of old Fort Bowyer, is a pentagonal, bastioned work, built of brick, whose full scarp wall is four feet, eight inches thick. It is located on the main land, at the west end of Mobile Point, and mounted, at the time of the passage of Farragut's fleet, eighty-six guns of various calibres, consisting of rifled thirty-twos, ten-inch columbiads, and two seven and eight-inch Brook's rifles. In each of its bastion-flanks were two smooth-bore twenty-four pounders. Twenty-nine additional guns were placed in exterior batteries, of which the most formidable, "the water battery," bore two rifled thirty-twos, four ten-inch columbiads, and one eight-inch Brook's rifle. Within the fort was a citadel, containing quarters for soldiers, whose brick walls, loop-holed for musketry, were four feet in thickness. The garrison of the fort, including officers and men, numbered six hundred and forty.

Fort Gaines, erected on the ruins of Fort Tombigbee, stands at the eastern extremity of Dauphine Island, three nautical miles in a west-northwest direction from Fort Morgan. It is built of brick, in the form of a star, with semi-detached scarp five feet thick, and small works, in angles, for flank defence. When invested by General Granger, it had forty-four gun-platforms laid, but upon only thirty of them were guns mounted, of which three were columbiads, and the rest thirty-two and twenty-four pounders. Its garrison consisted of forty-six officers and eight hundred and eighteen men.

On the flats, to the southward and eastward of Fort Gaines, innumerable piles were driven, to obstruct the passage of small vessels, and from these, two lines of torpedoes extended toward Fort Morgan, whose eastern limit was marked by a large red buoy. The channel between this and the fort was left open for blockade-runners, and, being but a few hundred yards wide, forced every vessel using it to pass close to the fort.

Such were the works, and such the means employed for guarding the main ship-channel; but, about six nautical miles northwest of Fort Gaines, there is a narrow cut for light-draught vessels, called Grant's Pass, which it was also deemed necessary to prevent the blockading fleet from getting possession of. For this purpose, between Cedar Point and Little Dauphine Island, on an islet of mostly made-land, covering an area of about half an acre, the Confederates had begun the construction of a redoubt, which they called Fort Powell. The front face of the work was nearly completed, and in a defensible condition, mounting one eight-inch columbiad, and one six- and four-tenths and two seven-inch Brook's rifles. The face looking toward Fort Gaines was about half finished, its parapets being nearly complete, while its galleries and traverses had only been framed. The rear face was without parapets, and the ten-inch columbiad and seven-inch Brook's rifle mounted there were exposed from the platform up. This part of the fort was encumbered with a large quantity of lumber, which was being used in the construction of galleries, magazines, &c.

Inside of these defences, to the northward of, and about five hundred yards distant from Fort Morgan, lay the iron-clad steamer Tennessee, two hundred and nine feet in length, and forty-eight feet broad, with an iron spur projecting beyond her bow, at a depth of two feet below the water-line, which made her, in public estimation, the most formidable ram of her time; yet, not trusting to *ramming* alone for victory, she carried in her casemate — whose sloping sides, covered with armor varying in thickness from five to six inches, were supposed to be impenetrable to shot — six Brook's rifled cannon. Of these, two were pivot and the others broadside guns, the former throwing solid projectiles of one hundred and ten pounds weight; the latter, solid projectiles of ninety-five pounds weight. The ports, of which there were ten, were so arranged that the pivot guns could be fought in broadside, sharp on the bow and quarter, and on a direct line with the keel. Her vital defect was her steering gear, which was badly arranged and much exposed. As but little is known, outside of the state of Alabama, of the *history* of this vessel, which bore the whole brunt of the battle on the Confederate side, after the Union fleet had fairly passed the forts, the following *resumé* of it cannot fail to prove interesting, I am sure, to the majority of my hearers assembled here to-night.* She was built at Selma, on the Alabama River, in the winter of 1863–64, and, so soon as her frame was put together, was towed to Mobile to receive her armor and armament, both of which, it is said, were made of iron taken from the ground early in 1863, at the very time that the timber was being cut in the forests, which, after passing through the hands of the shipwright, was used in the construction of her hull. About four months were consumed in putting on her plating, and this made her mean draught of water a little less than thirteen feet.

On her trial trip, in March, 1864, her speed was set down at eight knots; "but this was afterward reduced to six, by the increased draught caused by her heavy battery and ammunition, and the supply of fuel required to be placed on board, after she was taken down the bay."

And now, the ram being ready, the great problem to solve was, how to get her over Dog River Bar, on which, at high tide, the depth of water was but eight feet. To effect this, long wooden tanks, or caissons, called, in nautical language, camels, were prepared, so fashioned as to fit tightly to the Tennessee's bottom. These were to be placed on either side of the vessel, sunk by being filled with water, and then lashed securely in their places with

---

* It must be remembered that this paper was prepared at the request of, and read before The Military Historical Society of Massachusetts, as stated in my preface.   F. A. P.

heavy chains, after which, the water being pumped out, they would rise by their buoyancy, and of course lift the ship with them, if the lashings held.

The camels were just pronounced by their designer ready for service, when they were fired and destroyed; yet, not discouraged thereby, the Confederates set to work with a will to fell trees for the making of others, which being successfully accomplished, the Tennessee, in May, 1864, was raised some seven feet out of water, and carried across the bar into Mobile Bay.

Near the Tennessee were anchored three wooden gunboats, viz., the Morgan, the Gaines, and the Selma. The Morgan carried one sixty-three hundred weight eight-inch gun, and five fifty-seven hundred weight thirty-two pounders; the Gaines, one eight-inch Brook's rifle, and five fifty-seven hundred weight thirty-two pounders; the Selma, three eight-inch Paixhans, and one old-fashioned heavy thirty-two pounder, converted to a rifle and banded at the breech, throwing a solid projectile weighing about sixty pounds.

. . . . . .

During the time that the Alabamians were putting their forts into the condition described above, and assembling their vessels, they were almost unmolested. A small squadron, it is true, had been dispatched, early in May, 1861, to blockade Mobile Bay,[5] which Fort Morgan "welcomed by displaying, under the Confederate flag, an United States ensign with its union down," and, after the capture of New Orleans, that squadron was augmented until it had reached the proportions of a fleet; but it was not until every stronghold on the Mississippi had fallen into our hands, and the Confederacy was thereby cut in twain, that the government seriously directed its attention to the reduction of Mobile.

Accordingly, on January 20, 1864, we find Farragut, who possessed all its confidence, making a reconnoissance of the defences of Mobile Bay, and thus writing of them to the Navy Department:

"I went in over the bar in the gunboat Octorora, Lieutenant-Commander Lowe, taking the Itasca in company as a precaution against accident. We passed up to Sand Island, and laid abreast of the light-house on it. The day was uncommonly fine, and the air very clear. We were distant from the forts three and three and a half miles, and could see everything distinctly. I am satisfied that if I had one iron-clad at this time I could destroy their whole force in the bay, and reduce the forts at my leisure, by co-operation with our land forces, — say five thousand men. We must have about two thousand five hundred men in the rear of each fort, to make regular approaches by land, and to prevent the garrison's receiving supplies and reinforcements; the fleet to run the batteries, and fight the flotilla in the bay.

"But without iron-clads, we should not be able to fight the enemy's vessels of that class with much prospect of success, as the latter would lie on the flats, where our ships could not go to destroy them. Wooden vessels can do nothing with them, unless by getting within one hundred or two hundred yards, so as to ram them or pour in a broadside.

"The iron-clad Nashville, I am told by a refugee, will not be ready before March; and he says Buchanan made a speech to his men, saying that as soon as she is finished, he will raise the blockade, &c. It is depressing to see how easily false reports circulate, and in what a state of alarm the community is kept by the most absurd rumors.[6] If the department could get one or two of the iron-clads here, it would put an end to this state of things, and restore confidence to the people of the ports now in our possession.

"I feel no apprehension about Buchanan's raising the blockade of Mobile; but with such a force as he has in the bay, it would be unwise to take in our wooden vessels, without the means of fighting the enemy on an equal footing.

"By reference to the chart, you will see how small a space there is for the ships to manœuvre."

Early in May, the Tennessee, having been floated upon camels, as we have said, over Dog River Bar, steamed across the bay in full view of the blockading fleet; and Farragut seems to have been greatly impressed with her warlike appearance. "Unless she fails in some particular," he reports to the department, "I fear it will be much more difficult to take Mobile than it would have been one week ago."

Day by day now, however, the rear-admiral's spirits rose, as fresh vessels reported to him, and on the 12th of July he issued general order number ten, wherein, after prescribing the manner, in which the ships shall be "stript for the conflict," he says:

"The vessels will run past the forts in couples, lashed side by side, as hereinafter designated. The flag-ship will lead, and steer from Sand Island north by east by compass, until abreast of Fort Morgan; then northwest half north until past the Middle Ground; then north by west; and the others, as designated in the drawing, will he (Banks) would have left, according to the last returns, a force of over thirty thousand effective men, with which to move against Mobile; to which he expected to add five thousand men from Missouri. 'If, however,' he continued, 'you think the force here stated too small to hold the territory regarded as necessary to hold, I would say, concentrate at least twenty-five thousand men of your present command for operations against Mobile; with these, and such other additions as I can give you from elsewhere, lose no time in making a demonstration, to be followed by an attack.'"

The defeat of Banks, however, inspirited the Confederates west of the Mississippi to such a degree, that they at once assumed the offensive; so that General Canby, Banks's successor, finding ample employment for all his forces in Arkansas and Louisiana, was unable to carry out Grant's instructions, especially as he had been compelled to send six thousand men of his command to Washington, then menaced by Early. Grant thereupon postponed his contemplated movement upon Mobile to a more convenient season, contenting himself, meanwhile, with sending an order to Canby to dispatch to Farragut the troops necessary to invest forts Gaines and Morgan. Circumstances, however, making it impossible for Canby to spare men enough to invest both forts at once, it was agreed, at Farragut's suggestion, that Gaines should be first invested.

For this purpose, on the afternoon of August 3d, fifteen hundred men were landed on Dauphine Island by the boats, and under cover of the guns of a flotilla commanded by Lieutenant-Commander J. C. P. DeKraft.

The troops, which consisted of detachments from the Seventy-seventh Illinois, Thirty-fourth Iowa, Ninety-sixth

Ohio, Third Maryland Dismounted Cavalry, and Cobb's Colored Regiment of Engineers, under the immediate orders of Brigadier-General McGinnis, and accompanied by General Gordon Granger as commander-in-chief, took up their march, the moment they reached the shore, for Fort Gaines, distant from them fifteen miles. Their progress through the heavy sand was slow and laborious, and when night shut in, with a drenching rain, so intense was the darkness that "three times the skirmish line got in rear of the main column." They pushed forward with spirit, however, until midnight, and then, at the word of command, threw themselves down on the wet ground without a murmur, and slept the sweet sleep of the weary, until awakened by the bugles of the morrow, when they resumed their march, and, before the day closed, were intrenched about the fort, their skirmish line being less than half a mile from it.

At sunrise, on the 5th, Fort Gaines opened fiercely upon the besiegers; but, an hour later, the sharp crack of its rifles was hushed by the loud, continuous roar of artillery on the opposite side of the channel, where the magnificent spectacle presented itself of Farragut's fleet, wreathed in smoke, — its leading vessels one sheet of fire from their starboard batteries, — forcing the passage of Fort Morgan.

. . . .

From the day general order number ten was promulgated, up to the very moment of conflict, the greatest activity had prevailed in the Union fleet, all of whose vessels had, in turn, visited Pensacola, (but a few hours' sail from Mobile,) to get ready for the fray. In the ships carrying spars, nothing above the topmasts was left stand-

THE BATTLE OF MOBILE BAY. 19

ing, and the Richmond had wisely struck and landed even her topmasts and topsail yards. On the outside of each vessel, in the wake of her engines and boilers, chain cables were ranged fore and aft, and, inside, sand bags were placed, from stem to stern, and from the berth to the spar deck; and, in short, every contrivance that Yankee ingenuity could suggest was resorted to for the protection of the vessels and their crews from shot and shell, from splinters and falling spars.

Farragut had fully intended to run into the bay on the day the troops were landed on Dauphine Island, but his design was frustrated by the non-arrival of the monitor Tecumseh, until the evening of August 4th, when she steamed in and took up her anchorage in the Sand Island channel, with her consorts, the Winnebago, Manhattan, and Chickasaw.

On the following morning, at four o'clock, the wooden vessels, which were anchored three miles and a half south-southeast of the iron-clads, commenced getting under way, and forming double column, or column of *twos lashed together*, the starboard vessels of which were the Brooklyn, Hartford, Richmond, Lackawanna, Monongahela, Ossipee, and Oneida; the port ones, the Octorora, Metacomet, Port Royal, Seminole, Kennebec, Itasca, and Galena.

The inboard and starboard waist and quarter boats of many of the vessels of the fleet had been left at Pensacola; the others were being carried (lowered to the water's edge), or towed, out of harm's way, on the port side of the column, with the exception of the little Loyal, the admiral's steam barge, which, with its saucy howitzer in the bows, was making its way into rebeldom unaided.

As the Brooklyn had four chase-guns, and was provided with a torpedo-catcher, Farragut, at the instance of his captains, had given her the lead. "They urged it upon me," he says in his report to the Secretary of the Navy, "because, in their judgment, the flag-ship ought not to be too much exposed. This I believe to be an error; for, apart from the fact that exposure is one of the penalties of rank in the navy, it will always be the aim of the enemy to destroy the flag-ship, and such attempt was very persistently made, but Providence did not permit it to be successful."

The Hartford, a vessel already of historic fame from her having borne the flag of Farragut at New Orleans, was destined to bear it again in triumph on this memorable occasion. She was a screw-ship of the second class, with full sail-power, and of nineteen hundred tons burden; her extreme length being two hundred and twenty-five feet, her greatest breadth of beam forty-four, and her mean draught of water, with everything in, sixteen feet three inches. Her engines were direct-acting, developing a speed of eight knots, and her greatest speed, under sail and steam combined; was eleven knots. Her armament consisted of eighteen nine-inch Dahlgrens, two one hundred-pounder Parrotts, and one thirty-pounder Parrott; and the whole weight of solid projectiles thrown by her at a broadside was nine hundred and eighty pounds.

The Brooklyn and the Richmond were sister ships to the Hartford; the Lackawanna and Monongahela about five hundred tons smaller; and, from the Monongahela, the vessels of the fleet gradually decreased in size and armament, until we reach the little Itasca,[7] of five hundred tons, with a battery of one eleven-inch gun, two thirty-two pounders, of fifty-seven hundred weight, two twenty-pounder Parrotts, and one twelve-pounder Dahlgren.

The Tecumseh and the Manhattan were single-turreted monitors of the burden of five hundred and fifty tons, whose extreme length was two hundred and twenty-five feet, and extreme beam forty-three feet. The diameter of their ten-inch turrets, in the clear, was twenty-one feet, and each turret carried two fifteen-inch guns. Their side-armor was five, their deck-armor two inches thick, and the height of their decks above water eighteen inches.

The Chickasaw and the Winnebago were not so heavily armored as their consorts, and differed from them in having two turrets each, and in their light draught of water, which was but six feet. In each of their turrets were mounted two eleven-inch guns.

The total weight of metal of the advancing fleet was fourteen thousand two hundred and forty-six pounds; that thrown by it at a broadside, nine thousand two hundred and eighty-eight pounds.

So soon as the vessels were in position, they hoisted an ensign at each mast-head, and steered for the Sand Island channel, the monitors joining them, as they crossed "the outer bar," and forming, in column of vessels, on their starboard side, abreast of the Brooklyn, Hartford, and Richmond.

The morning was a beautiful one, the sea smooth, and the sky unclouded; and, as the fleet steamed steadily up the main ship-channel, — drum answering drum from van to rear, in hoarse summons to the officers and men of each ship to assemble at their quarters, — De Kraft, who was watching it from the mast-head of the Conemaugh, was struck with its "stately appearance and compact order." "I noticed also, with great satisfaction," he remarks, "that a light breeze was springing up from the westward, which must certainly blow the smoke from our guns, as soon as they opened, full upon the fort and batteries."

At six o'clock, the Confederate vessels, upon signal from their admiral, emerged from behind the fort, and took position, in single echelon, across the channel, with their port batteries bearing upon our fleet. The Selma, on the right, was in advance, and farthest to the northward; while the ram Tennessee, on the left, rested a little to the westward of the red buoy, and close to the inner line of torpedoes, upon which, as the tide was flood, there was no danger of her drifting.

About this time, too, the steamers Gennesseo, Pinola, Pembina, Sebago, Tennessee, and Bienville came to anchor to the southward and eastward of Fort Morgan, and opened fire upon it. The station assigned to them was to the northward of the *Southeast Shoal*, as close to Mobile Point as they could get, so that they might, in a measure, keep down the fire of the fort, while the fleet was passing it; but through some misunderstanding, perhaps, on the part of their senior officer, Lieutenant-Commander Grafton, they were anchored at such a respectful distance from the shore as to render their fire useless.

At forty-seven minutes past six, the Tecumseh, which was then in the lead, about three hundred yards from the Brooklyn and sharp on her starboard bow, fired her guns, merely for the purpose of scaling them, and then loaded each with sixty pounds of powder and a steel shot, in readiness to engage the ram.

At six minutes past seven, the fort opened, and was replied to by the Brooklyn, and, in a few minutes thereafter, the action became general on both sides.

The scene from the Conemaugh was now grand beyond all description : the forts, batteries, and monitors enveloped in smoke, made luminous by the flashes of their guns; the wooden vessels in plain view, vomiting fire from stem to stern; and the grand old admiral in the port main rigging of the Hartford, just below the futtock staff, reclining, as it were, in a sort of bridle or swing passed around his back and under his arms, whose ends were fastened to the futtock shrouds, — one hand grasped the rigging, and in the other he held a marine glass; and thus, without danger of losing his hold or footing, he could turn easily in every direction, and see all that was passing below him, on the water and on the land.

Beneath him, on the poop, was his fleet-captain, Percival Drayton, an officer noted for his professional ability and zeal for the service ; and, in the top above his head, leaning against the rail, stood his trusty pilot, Martin Freeman, whose services should ever be remembered with gratitude by the republic. Communicating, through a speaking-tube, with the deck of the Hartford, and signalling with his hands to the commanding officer of her consort, Lieutenant-Commander Jouett, who stood on the starboard wheel-house of his vessel, he piloted the flag-ship, amid all the vicissitudes of battle, with a calmness and intrepidity truly heroic.

And indeed, throughout the whole fleet, a spirit of devotion to duty was manifested worthy of the descendants of the men who had blown up the Philadelphia in the harbor of Tripoli, followed Perry and McDonough on lakes Erie and Champlain, and burned a Mexican schooner moored to the castle of San Juan D'Ulloa.

The signal quartermaster, with his flags at hand, kept his glass steadily fixed upon the flag-ship. What cared he for shot or shell, if the signals of the admiral were but truly transmitted or replied to?

The helmsman, with his hands grasping the spokes of the wheel, had ears alone for his captain and the pilot. "*Starboard a little!*" "*Port a little!*" he cried from time to time, echoing the orders of his superiors.

The leadsmen in the chains gave out their soundings as coolly and deliberately as if they were entering a friendly harbor, and, mingling with the cries of the helmsman, as the water shoaled, came their warning words, "*By the mark, three!*" or, "*A quarter less four!*" in the musical tones so dear to seamen.

The bronzed veteran and the old salt who had seen service in Mexico and China stood side by side, at the guns, with the young marine officer and the boy-graduate of the academy, and each had equal faith in the other; for all knew that to die for one's country, when need be, is not only "sweet and decorous," but strictly according to navy teaching, and "the usage of the sea-service."

And in this faith all went to their posts, prepared to obey the regulations and "fight courageously;" for, in a fleet where a single shell, exploding in the boiler of a vessel, might subject the engineers and firemen to the fate of Marsyas, or a torpedo or infernal, exploding under her bottom, send all hands journeying *ad astra*, no one could properly be considered a non-combatant.

The *morale* of the Union fleet, then, was what the French would call superb; all, from the highest to the lowest, placing implicit faith in Farragut, and all prepared to take any risks when led by him. Thus, while the captain of the Winnebago was coolly walking back and forth on the bridge of his vessel, giving orders, first to the gunners of one turret, then to those of the other, how to direct their fire, a negro seaman, probably stationed at the life buoy, was as coolly promenading the poop-deck of the Galena. Seemingly unconscious of all that was passing around him, this man, with his hands uplifted to heaven, was loudly singing a negro hymn. God knows what thoughts were passing through his mind on this *his* day of jubilee!

At a quarter past seven, the flag-ship signalled to the wooden vessels, *closer order*, when the column was closed as compactly as possible, the bows of each pair of vessels being within a few yards of the vessels next ahead, and a little on their starboard quarter.

The fleet was now heading a point to the left of Fort Morgan, its rear being past Sand Island, and the van within half a mile of the water battery, whose galling fire, as well as that of the Confederate squadron, could only be replied to by the bow-chasers of its leading vessels.

By half past seven, the Tecumseh, which still maintained her position ahead of the Brooklyn, was well up with the fort, and drawing slowly by the Tennessee, leaving her on the port beam.

At this moment, when the eyes of all were riveted upon the iron-clads, expecting to see them hotly engaged so soon as the Tecumseh should have passed the lines of torpedoes intervening between them, the Brooklyn and the Hartford poured a broadside into Fort Morgan, driving the enemy, helter-skelter, from their barbette and water batteries.

The sight was an inspiriting one, and, in the enthusiasm of the moment, the gallant Craven, who thirsted for the honor of engaging the ram singly, gave the fatal order, *Hard a-starboard!* and dashed straight at her, *his course taking him to the westward of the large red buoy.*

The bow gun of the Tennessee, loaded with a steel bolt weighing one hundred and forty pounds, was kept steadily trained upon the monitor as she advanced. "Do not fire, Mr. Wharton," cried Captain Johnston, of the Tennessee, to the lieutenant in charge of her first division, "until the vessels are in actual contact." "Aye, aye, sir," was the cool response of Wharton, as he stepped to the breech of the bow gun, "in expectation of a deadly fight at close quarters." Scarce were the words uttered, when the Tecumseh, reeling to port as from an earthquake shock, foundered, head foremost, with almost every soul on board, destroyed by a torpedo.[8] A few of her crew were observed to leap wildly from her turret; for an instant her screw was seen revolving in air — and then there was nothing left to show that the Tecumseh had ever formed one of that proud Union fleet but a small boat washed from her deck, and a number of half-drowned men struggling fiercely for life in the seething waters which had closed over their vessel forever.

Such was the fate of the Tecumseh!

Short shrift had they who went down with her! Yet, short as the time of her foundering was, it has furnished us with one of those magnificent episodes of war which make famous the annals of nations.

Craven and Mr. John Collins, the pilot of the Tecumseh, met, as their vessel was sinking beneath them, at the foot of the ladder leading to the top of the turret.

Great and good men often err; but they differ from ordinary mortals in this, that they are willing to atone for their errors, even with their lives, if necessary. It may be, then, that Craven, in the nobility of his soul, — for all know he was one of nature's noblemen, — it may be, I say, that in the nobility of his soul, the thought flashed across him that it was through no fault of his pilot that the Tecumseh was in this peril: he drew back. "After you, pilot," said he, grandly.

"There was nothing after me," relates Mr. Collins, who fortunately lived to tell this tale of heroism; "when I reached the upmost round of the ladder, the vessel seemed to drop from under me."

Yet Craven's words, carried to Heaven by approving angels as evidence of man's *humanity* to man, will live forever in the book of life, with no tear on the page to efface the record.

Therefore the navy points with exultation — not regret — to the buoy off Fort Morgan, which watches over his iron tomb.

> "His sword is rust,
> His body dust,
> His soul is with the saints, we trust."
>
> . . . . .
> . . . . .

Beholding the disaster to the Tecumseh, the Brooklyn stopped. "What is the matter with the Brooklyn?" asked the admiral, anxiously; "Freeman, she must have plenty of water there."

"Plenty of water, and to spare, admiral," replied the

sturdy pilot; "but her screw is moving: I think she is going ahead again, sir."

Ahead again! If that were true, it were glorious news indeed! But no! By heaven, she backs! backs full upon the flag-ship; thus arresting the advance of the whole fleet; so that the rear presses upon the van, the van upon the rear, and all is disorder and confusion.

The enemy, not slow to comprehend this condition of affairs, take advantage of their opportunity, and, manning all the guns from which they have so recently been driven, pour in a murderous fire upon our fleet, which meets with but a feeble fire in return.

"At this critical moment," writes an eye-witness, "the batteries of our ships were almost silent, while the whole of Mobile Point was a living line of flame." The slightest vacillation then on the part of the admiral, and the battle would have been lost, and the greater part of the fleet destroyed.

But Farragut was equal to the emergency. His great qualities as a commander, which were apparent to all who were near him in times of *extreme* peril, were never more conspicuous than on this trying occasion. Danger there was, and disaster there might be ahead, he knew; but astern were sure defeat and dishonor; and for America's great admiral — the man who was born to be a hero — there could be but one course to steer, that leading straight into Mobile Bay, where the Confederate vessels were awaiting him.

But between him and the Confederates interposed the Brooklyn, and how to get by her was the question; for she lay right athwart the Hartford's hawse, bows on to Fort Morgan.

Then was made manifest the soundness of the admiral's judgment in lashing his vessels together by pairs; for the Hartford going ahead, while the Metacomet backed, the bows of the former were swung to the westward, until clear of the Brooklyn's stern, when both vessels gathered headway. As they were slowly passing the Brooklyn, her captain reported "a heavy line of torpedoes across the channel."

"Damn the torpedoes!" was the emphatic reply of Farragut. "Jouett, full speed! Four bells, Captain Drayton." And the Hartford, as if eager to bear the admiral's flag to the front, bounded forward "like a thing of life," and, increasing her speed at each instant, crossed both lines of torpedoes, going over the ground at the rate of nine miles an hour; for so far had she drifted to the northward and westward while her engines were stopped, as to make it impossible for the admiral, without heading directly *on* to Fort Morgan, to obey his own instructions to "pass eastward of the easternmost buoy."

As soon as he could get his vessel's head to the northward, Alden, the captain of the Brooklyn, "pushed up the channel at full speed, in the Hartford's wake," and, during the fight which ensued with the Confederate ram, displayed his usual gallantry. A good seaman, a skilful officer, whose battle-record attests his bravery, his hesitancy at "Mobile's Gate" must needs be ascribed to an error of judgment, since all will admit that in many a stubborn fight elsewhere he served the Republic well.

． ． ． ． ． ． ．

While "the guardian of the fleet," as one of the officers who served under him appropriately styles Farragut, was engaged in extricating it from its perilous position, he was not unmindful of the survivors of the Tecumseh, whom he beheld in the water near by. "Send a boat, Jouett," said he. "and pick up the poor fellows." Jouett, in expectation of the order, had already dispatched a boat on this humane mission, in charge of Acting Ensign (now Lieutenant-Commander) Henry C. Nields. Starting from the port quarter of the Metacomet, and steering the boat himself, this mere boy pulled directly under the battery of the Hartford, and around the Brooklyn, to within a few hundred yards of the fort, exposed to the fire of both friends and foes.

After he had gone a little distance from his vessel, he seemed suddenly to reflect that he had no flag flying, when he dropped the yoke-ropes, picked up a small ensign from the bottom of the boat, and, unfurling it from its staff, which he shipped in a socket made for it in the stern-sheets, he threw it full to the breeze, amid the loud cheers of his men. "I can scarcely describe," says an officer of the Tennessee, "how I felt at witnessing this most gallant act. The muzzle of our gun was slowly raised, and the bolt intended for the Tecumseh flew harmlessly over the heads of that glorious boat's crew, far down in the line of our foes."

After saving Ensign Zetlich, eight men, and the pilot, Nields turned, and pulling for the fleet, succeeded in reaching the Oneida, where he remained until the close of the action..

. . . .

The order of battle being restored, through Farragut's indomitable pluck and decision of character, the Union fleet sped swiftly by Fort Morgan, each vessel, as she got fairly abreast of the fort, pouring into it such a shower of shell, shrapnel, grape, and canister as, for the time, completely silenced its batteries; and although many of the vessels were repeatedly hulled by the enemy's missiles, as they drew near to or receded from the fort, yet all escaped serious damage, with the exception of the Oneida, which, being the starboard rear vessel of the column, was exposed to the concentrated fire of every gun on Mobile Point not previously dismounted or disabled.[9]

She was almost by the fort, however, when a rifled shell passed through her chain armor, and entering the starboard boiler exploded in it, causing sad havoc among the firemen and coal-heavers of the watch below, all of whom were either killed outright or fearfully scalded by the escaping steam. Another shell, exploding in the cabin, cut both wheel-ropes, while a third set fire to the deck above the forward magazine; yet, encouraged by the chivalric bearing of their commander, and the fine example set them by the executive officer and the chief engineer of the ship, the crew of the Oneida behaved splendidly. The relieving tackles were instantly manned, the fire put out, and connection between the starboard and port boiler cut off; and the Oneida, assisted by the Galena, went on as if nothing unusual had happened on board of her, her guns never for a moment ceasing to respond to the really terrific fire of the enemy.

When she got beyond the range of the fort, De Kraft signalled to his flotilla to get under way, and approaching Fort Powell as near as the depth of water would permit, anchored his vessels in the form of a crescent, and commenced a vigorous bombardment of the fort, which the Confederates spiritedly replied to.

· · · · · · · ·

As the Hartford entered Mobile Bay, the ram "dashed out" at her, and failing to overtake her, turned and made for the Brooklyn, Richmond, and Lackawanna in succession, but missed them all, saluting each, however, as she went by, with a broadside, which did great injury to the vessel, and laid many a brave fellow low, while their fire, in reply, made not the slightest impression on her iron shield.

Then Strong, in the Monongahela, determined to resort to ramming, and, getting a good position on the Tennessee's beam, he attempted, at full speed, to run her down.

The Tennessee, to avoid being struck amidships, put her helm a-starboard, and the two vessels collided at an acute angle, the ram swinging alongside of the Monongahela's consort, the Kennebec, whose sharp cutwater cut her barge in two.

As she lay close aboard of the Kennebec, she succeeded in exploding a shell on that vessel's berth-deck, which killed and wounded several of her officers and men, carried away all her ladders, and so filled the ship with smoke that she was supposed to be on fire, and the alarm sounded. This created some excitement among the crew; which was quickly allayed, however, by the calm, cool conduct of her commanding and other officers.

Passing the Ossipee without firing a gun at her, the ram next steered for the crippled Oneida, and shooting under her stern, fired two broadsides at her in rapid succession, which destroyed her boats and cabin furniture, cut away the greater part of her lower rigging, damaged her mainmast and one of the heavy gun-carriages, and dismounted the twelve-pound howitzer on the poop.

Fortunately the enemy fired high, or there would have

been few left on board the Oneida to tell the story of her engagement with the dreaded ram. Among the wounded was the gallant Mullany, who had volunteered for the fight, and throughout the whole of it given to his officers and crew "a noble example of unflinching courage and heroism."

It was now at an end, so far as the Oneida was concerned, which shortly afterward came to anchor well up the bay, while the Tennessee sought the shelter of Fort Morgan.[10]

During the time that their flag-ship was engaged in her work of destruction, the Confederate gunboats were far from idle. From their position ahead of the Hartford they had been enabled to keep up a most destructive fire upon her, "a single shot from the Selma killing ten and wounding five men at numbers one and two guns." At a little past eight, however, the admiral, observing that all his vessels were clear of the fort, made signal, — *Gunboats chase enemy's gunboats.* The signal was hardly above the Hartford's deck, when Jouett, cutting the fasts which bound him to that vessel, started in obedience to it, followed, at some distance, by the Itasca, Kennebec, and Port Royal.

The Confederates had no course open to them but retreat, keeping up a heavy fire from their stern guns as they fled. A violent rain squall coming on just then, the Gaines was enabled to seek the cover of the fort, which she reached in a sinking condition, her commanding officer running her on shore, and setting fire to her, to prevent her falling into Union hands.

At nine o'clock, "the Morgan hauled off to starboard," and, at ten minutes past nine, the Selma struck her flag to the Metacomet.[11] She had been well defended. Two of her officers and six of her men were killed, and the number of her wounded amounted to ten, among whom was her captain, Lieutenant-Commander Murphy.

. . . .

And now, having witnessed with admiration and pride the heroism of the Union fleet in entering Mobile Bay, despite Fort Morgan, the Confederate squadron, and the torpedoes so thickly strewed in its way, we shall contemplate with hardly less pride, and with similar admiration, I am sure, the heroic daring of our brothers in arms on board the Tennessee, who, when the forts were passed, and the Confederate gunboats dispersed, resolved unaided to attempt the forlorn hope of wresting victory from three iron-clads and fourteen wooden vessels.[12]

So soon as the Tennessee reached Fort Morgan, her armor was carefully examined and found intact, while not an officer or man on board of her was injured in the slightest degree, a few shot-holes in her smoke-stack alone telling of her conflict with the Union fleet: these were soon patched, and she steered once more for the Hartford, now lying quietly at anchor about three miles away.

The moment Farragut saw her coming, he signalled to his monitors and largest wooden vessels "to attack the ram, not only with their guns, but bows on at full speed; and then began one of the fiercest naval combats on record."

The Monongahela, not having anchored, was the first to make a rush at her, going through the water at full ten miles an hour; yet so bent was Admiral Buchanan on the Hartford's destruction, that he entirely ignored every other vessel, not deigning to take the slightest notice of the Monongahela's approach until she was close aboard of him, on his port beam. Then he ordered the Tennessee's helm a-port, which caused the Monongahela to strike her at a slightly oblique angle; nevertheless the shock of the collision was such that many of the crews of both vessels measured their lengths on their respective decks. "The Tennessee," writes Lieutenant Wharton, "yielded to the impact, and spun swiftly round, as upon a pivot. I felt as if I were going through the air. 'What is the matter, Captain Johnston?' I asked. 'We've been rammed, sir,' was the response from the pilot-house, where he stood."

During the instant of actual contact, the ram fired two shots at her antagonist, piercing her through and through, while the Monongahela's whole broadside, discharged at the casemate of the ram, rolled harmlessly down its sloping sides.

"The Monongahela was hardly clear of us," says Wharton again, "when a hideous-looking monster came creeping up on our port side, whose slowly revolving turret revealed the cavernous depths of a mammoth gun. *Stand clear of the port side!* I shouted. A moment after, a thundering report shook us all, while a blast of dense, sulphurous smoke covered our port-holes, and four hundred and forty pounds of iron, impelled by sixty pounds of powder, admitted daylight through our side, where, before it struck us, there had been over two feet of solid wood, covered with five inches of solid iron. This was the only fifteen-inch shot that hit us fair. It did not come through; the inside netting caught the splinters, and there were no casualties from it. I was glad to find myself alive after that shot."

The Lackawanna next bore down upon the Tennessee, and although her stern was stove in to the plank ends, "for the distance of three feet above the water line to five feet below it," no perceptible effect was produced on the ram, beyond giving her a slight list, from which she quickly righted, going on as before, and always heading for the Hartford. Nor did the Hartford shun the encounter; but, following closely in the Lackawanna's wake, she too struck the Tennessee a fearful blow, at the same time throwing her whole port broadside full upon the casemate of the ram, which, like the Monongahela's broadside, failed to injure it in the slightest degree.

Surrounded as she was by enemies, the ram had this advantage, that she could fire or run at every vessel in view, while the Unionists had to be careful not to fire at or come in collision with their own vessels. Indeed, it so happened that the Hartford, while making for the ram a second time, was run into by the Lackawanna, and cut down to within two feet of the water's edge.

Thus, for an hour or more, the Tennessee contended successfully against the whole Union fleet; but, at the expiration of that hour, it became evident to all on board of her that victory was impossible and defeat certain, unless she could get a second time under the protection of Fort Morgan, for which Captain Johnston, in obedience to Buchanan's orders, then steered.

But by this time, to use the language of Farragut, "she was sore beset." The Manhattan was hanging on her starboard quarter, pounding her with fifteen-inch solid and cored shot; the Winnebago, not far off, saluting her with eleven-inch steel bolts; and the wooden vessels ramming her, one after the other, in quick succession, "with a reckless daring worthy of success." But the vessel that undoubtedly inflicted the most injury upon the ram was the monitor Chickasaw, commanded by Lieutenant-Commander George H. Perkins, "which hung," said the pilot of the Tennessee, "close under our stern. Move as we would, she was always there, firing the two eleven-inch guns in her forward turret like pocket-pistols, so that she soon had the plates flying in the air."

Thus, "stormed at by shot and shell," and rammed, every few minutes, by a heavy vessel going at great speed, with three of her wrought-iron port-shutters jammed while half closed, and her steering-apparatus,[13] relieving tackles, and smoke-stack shot away, the Tennessee lay, at last, like a log upon the water, — a mere target for her foes.

Then Captain Johnston, repairing to the berth deck, where Admiral Buchanan was lying, under the surgeon's hands, with a fractured leg, sorrowfully reported to the admiral that resistance was no longer possible. "Do the best you can, Johnston," was Buchanan's reply, "and when all is done, surrender."

When Johnston returned to the pilot-house, he beheld the Ossipee approaching at full speed, while the fire of our vessels was each instant increasing in intensity. The Tennessee had *already* done her best, and there was no time for dilly-dallying; so, hastening to the top of "the shield," which was exposed to a perfect shower of solid projectiles, this truly brave man hauled down the Confederate ensign with his own hands. — It had been raised in triumph, it was lowered without dishonor.[14]

The captured officers and men were transferred to the

Ossipee, and soon afterward sent to Pensacola; and it is pleasant to know that, to this day, they speak warmly of the hospitality extended to them by their captors.

． ． ． ． ． ． ． ．

It will be remembered that, while this fierce naval fight was taking place in Mobile Bay, De Kraft's flotilla, anchored in Grant's Pass, was busily engaged shelling Fort Powell. During the morning, although the fort was hit several times, no particular damage was done to it; but, about two in the afternoon, the Chickasaw, steaming up to within seven hundred yards of its eastern face, commenced a rapid fire with shell and grape, which the enemy was only able to reply to with a single Brook's rifle. A shell, entering one of the sally-ports, passed entirely through the bomb-proof, and buried itself, without exploding, in the opposite wall; another, and another following, burst in the face of the fort, displacing the sand so rapidly that Lieutenant-Colonel Williams, its commandant, became convinced that it would soon be rendered untenable. He therefore telegraphed to Colonel Anderson, commanding Fort Gaines, *Unless I can evacuate, I will be compelled to surrender within forty-eight hours.*

Anderson's reply was, *Save your garrison when your fort is no longer tenable.* At the time this despatch was received, it was growing dark, and the Lieutenant-Colonel instantly decided that it would be better to save his command, and destroy the fort, than to allow both to fall into the enemy's hands. The fleet had not yet moved up to intercept his communications, the tide was low, and he could not expect to find another such favorable opportunity for escaping; so he silently withdrew, leaving Lieutenants Savage and Jeffers to spike the guns, and blow up the fort so soon as he should make signal to them that its garrison had reached the main land. This signal was made about 10.30 P. M., just as De Kraft and Lieutenant-Commander Franklin, who had arrived during the day with a mail for the fleet, were returning to the Conemaugh in a small gig from a visit to the victorious admiral.

"Now, to find Grant's Pass at night," writes De Kraft, "it was necessary to steer directly for Fort Powell, which loomed up boldly against the clear sky. When within half a mile of it, a bright port-fire was observed to burn for a few seconds; then a dark column rose suddenly to a great height, and a heavy report and vivid flash announced that Fort Powell had been blown up."

About daylight the next morning, Lieutenant-Colonel Williams marched into Mobile with every officer and man of his command, consisting of two infantry companies of the Thirty-first Alabama, and a detachment of Culpepper's Battery, in all about one hundred and forty souls.[15]

At the same time, Acting Volunteer Lieutenant Pomeroy, commanding the Estrella, hoisted the stars and stripes over the ruins of the fort, and a large force was set to work to remove the obstructions in Grant's Pass, which being soon effected, direct communication by water was once more established between Mobile Bay and New Orleans.

. . . .

During the morning of the 6th of August, the fleet was occupied in repairing damages; but on the afternoon of that day it began to make preparations for a general bombardment of Fort Gaines on the morrow, the Chickasaw getting under way a little before sunset, and dropping several shells into it, as a forerunner of what was to follow.

The besieging army meanwhile had mounted two thirty-pounder Parrotts and four twelve-pounder rifles, and was hard at work laying down platforms for new guns.

But Admiral Farragut, knowing full well the fort could not hold out long against such a fire as would be brought to bear upon it, and anxious to spare the further effusion of blood, sent a flag-of-truce boat to the fort, as soon as the Chickasaw withdrew from it, with a request that Colonel Anderson and his staff would come to see him on board the Hartford. Colonel Anderson accepted the invitation, and was accompanied by Major Brown, and both were very kindly received by the admiral in his cabin.

There were present at this interview, beside the admiral and the two Confederate officers, Major-General Gordon Granger, Captain Percival Drayton, and Major James E. Montgomery, Assistant-Adjutant-General and Chief of Staff of the thirteenth army corps.

The admiral then said to Colonel Anderson that he had sent for him to advise the immediate surrender of the fort. "Surrounded on three sides by my vessels, and on the fourth by the army," said he, "you cannot possibly hold it. Submit, then, like a man to this hard necessity, and prevent further loss of life."

Anderson at once saw the force of the admiral's advice, and appreciated its humanity; but Major Brown demurred, and wanted to "fight it out," when Farragut told him he could understand his feelings, and was the last man to advise a surrender as long as there was a hope of preventing it; adding, with much feeling, "Gentlemen, if hard fighting could save that fort, I would advise you to fight to the death; but, by all the laws of war, you have not even a *chance* of saving it." The major admitted it was a forlorn hope, and finally agreed with his colonel that the surrender was necessary, and it was then and there agreed that it should take place on the following morning, at nine o'clock.

The officers took a glass of wine together, and signed the surrender, and the meeting broke up, Captain Drayton and Major Montgomery being appointed by their respective chiefs to take possession of the fort on the morrow, in the name of the army and navy of the United States.

Accordingly, at nine A. M. of the 7th, Drayton and Montgomery were admitted into the fort, and, an hour or two later, the besieging army, conducted by Montgomery, appeared before its walls. Then the garrison marched out and stacked their arms, and the officers delivered up their swords, and Fort Gaines passed into Federal hands, striking its flag to the Navy.

The Confederates were now embarked in transports and sent to New Orleans, while the Union troops, finding in the fort a large quantity of supplies, "regaled themselves," according to Andrews, "with the best meal they had had since arriving on Dauphine Island, — corndodgers, fried bacon, and coffee."

Immediately after the surrender of Fort Gaines, Fort Morgan was formally summoned by the admiral and General Granger, the message from the former being delivered in person to General Page, who commanded it, by Lieutenant J. Crittenden Watson, that of the latter by Major Montgomery. But General Page expressed his determination to defend his post to the last extremity, and preparations were therefore at once made by the combined forces to reduce it.

"On the 9th, at daylight, General Granger's command, now re-enforced by the Twentieth Wisconsin, Thirty-eighth Iowa, and Ninety-fourth Illinois, embarked for Navy Cove, four miles from Fort Morgan, on the bay side." From this point they gradually advanced, until, by the 21st, — a siege train having previously arrived under Brigadier-General Richard Arnold, — the land forces had sixteen mortars and twenty-five cannon in position, within five hundred yards of the fort, the naval battery of four nine-inch Dahlgrens, manned by seamen taken from the Hartford, Brooklyn, Richmond, and Lackawanna, and commanded by Lieutenant H. B. Tyson, being of the number.

At daylight on the 22d, the monitors and other vessels of the fleet took the stations assigned them north, south, and west of the fort, — the army being on the east, — so that it was completely invested. Then began one of the most furious bombardments that sailor or soldier has ever witnessed. It continued all day long without intermission, but after sunset began to slacken, until, by nine at night, it had become slow and irregular. Just then, however, a bright light shot up from the centre of the fort, and it was discovered that the citadel was on fire, when the besiegers sprung with renewed vigor to their guns, whose never-ceasing flashes fairly illumined the sky — six or eight mortar-shells could be seen in the air at once, while the thunder of the artillery was heard even in Mobile.

Yet amid all the horrors of this disastrous night, with

their walls breached, almost every piece of ordnance disabled, and the magazines endangered by the conflagration, which raged fiercely for several hours, the garrison of Fort Morgan was not dismayed. Some of the soldiers applied themselves to throwing their powder into the cisterns, others to spiking or destroying dismounted guns, while others again contended successfully with the devouring flames. Among these, Privates Murphy, Benbough, and Stevens, of the First Tennessee, were especially commended by their general "for great courage and daring displayed."

As day dawned, the citadel was again set on fire, and burned until it was consumed. To resist longer would have been madness, and at six A. M. a white flag was displayed upon the parapet of the fort, when the firing of the Unionists ceased.

At two in the afternoon the ceremony of surrender took place, and the brave garrison, whose loss had been between fifty and sixty in killed and wounded, was sent to New Orleans in the steamers Bienville and Tennessee.

Thus the Confederate banner disappeared from view, and the whole of Mobile Bay was ours.

Yet, remembering that of the actors in this strife all were Americans, we glory not in our brothers' defeat, rejoice not in our victory, save as these have tended to the restoration of the Union.

God grant that when the next war comes, in every fight, whether by land or by sea, we may stand shoulder to shoulder and side by side, with the star-spangled banner — the emblem of equal rights to all — waving above our heads, and not one single *sectional* flag to be seen upon the battle-field.

God grant, too, that Farragut's name may ever be revered by his countrymen, and that, in remembrance of his glorious services, his patriotism, and his valor, the old Hartford be preserved by us, as the great English nation preserves Nelson's flag-ship, the Victory.[16]

NOTES.

Note 1. (Page 7.)

Mauvila era Lugar fortificado. Tenia ochenta casas, aunque en cada una cabian mil Hombres: estaba en un llano, cercado de Maderas hincados, i otros atrevesados con Paja larga, i unas Quebrados, i Tierra, con que se hinchian los huecos, de manera, que parecia Muralla, ò Pared enlucida con Llana de Albañir, i à cada ochenta pasos havia una Torre, adonde podian pelear ocho Hombres, i havia muchas Saeteras con dos puertas, i enmedio de el Lugar havia una gran Plaça. — HERRERA.

Note 2. (Page 7.)

Tascaluça, sabiendo, por sus correos, que el Governador venia cerca, salio a recebirle fuera del Pueblo. Estava en un cerrillo alto, lugar eminente, de donde a todas partes se descubria mucha tierra. Tenia en su compañia no mas de cien hombres Nobles, muy bien adereçados de ricas mantas de diversos aforros, con grandes plumages en las cabeças conforme el trage, y usança dellas. Todos estavan en pie, solo Tascaluça estava sentado en una silla, de las que los Señores de aquellas tierras usan, que son de madera, una tercia, poco mas, ó menos de alto, con algun concavo, para el asiento, sin espaldar, ni braçeras, toda de una pieça. Cabe si tenia un Alferez con un gran Estandarte hecho de gamuça amarilla, con tres barras açules que lo partian de una parte a otra, hecho al mismo talle, y forma de los Estandartes que en España traen las Compañias de Cavallos.

Fue cosa nueva para los Españoles, vèr Insignia Militar, porque hasta entonces no avian visto, Estandarte, Vandera, ni Guion. — GARCILASO DE LA VEGA.

NOTE 3. (Page 7.)

El Capitan Diego de Soto llegó a lo mas recio de la batalla, y apenas havia entrado en ella, quando le dieron un flechaço por un ojo, que se salio al colodrillo, de que cayó luego en tierra, y sin habla estuvo agoniçando hasta otro dia, que murió sin que huviesen podido quitarle la flecha. Esta fue la vengança que hiço à su pariente Don Carlos, para mayor dolor, y perdida del General, y de todo el Exercito, porque eran dos Cavalleros, que dignamente merecian ser Sobrinos de tal Tio. — GARCILASO.

NOTE 4. (Page 8.)

Fort Morgan, at the entrance of Mobile Bay, was taken this morning by Alabama troops, and is now garrisoned by two hundred men. — THE PRESS, *January* 5, 1861.

The United States arsenal at Mobile was taken by the secessionists at daylight, this morning. It contained six stand of arms, fifteen hundred barrels of powder, three hundred thousand rounds of musket-cartridges, and other munitions of war. There was no defence. — EVENING POST, *January* 7, 1861.

NOTE 5. (Page 12.)

The *Natchez Courier* of to-day says: "Fort Morgan welcomed the blockading fleet by displaying the United States flag, with the Union down, from the same staff, and below the Confederate flag. — *May* 27, 1861.

Note 6. (Page 14.)

Of these "absurd rumors" the following is a specimen:

Chicago, *Thursday, July* 31, (1863.) The *Times* has a special despatch, dated Memphis, 28th instant, which says: "Late advices from the South, by rebel sources, are important. Ten ironclad gunboats, built in England, and fully equipped, have arrived off Mobile harbor, and three more are on their way. These constitute a fleet, ordered by the Southern Confederacy, and purchased in Europe. They mount from ten to thirty guns each, and are said to be mailed with six-inch iron. The blockade was run openly, by the dint of superior strength and weight of metal. Mobile is now considered open to the commerce of the world, with the support of the newly-acquired power."

Note 7. (Page 20.)

While the Itasca was passing Fort Morgan, her commanding officer, Lieutenant-Commander George Brown, was struck by a splinter, which caused him for some moments great pain. "What is the matter, Brown?" asked the executive officer of the Ossipee; "have you been struck by a splinter?" "You may call it a splinter on your big vessel," roared Brown, in reply; "but aboard this little craft it *ranks as a log of wood.*"

Note 8. (Page 26.)

A curious incident of the passage of Fort Morgan is related by several officers:

When the Tecumsch went down, the crew of the Hartford sprung upon her starboard hammock rail, and gave three loud, defiant cheers. This cheering was mistaken, by the crews of the vessels following the Hartford, as an indication of some advantage gained over the enemy, and taken up by them in succession.

"I hailed the Lackawanna," says Captain McCann, who commanded the Kennebec, "to learn the cause of the prolonged cheering. '*The Tecumseh has sunk the Tennessee!*' some one replied, and in an instant, *my* men were cheering as enthusiastically as the others."

Note 9. (Page 31.)

"Not to have made mistakes," says Jomini, "is never to have commanded;" yet the only *flaw* in Farragut's order of battle seems to have been his permitting the Oneida to bring up the rear. Our experience during the civil war showed that, in passing forts and batteries, the last vessel invariably got "peppered;" therefore, the starboard rear vessel of the column should have been one whose broadside was to be dreaded. Had the Richmond, for instance, whose fire is particularly commended "for precision, accuracy, and rapidity," been in the Oneida's place, the whole fleet would probably have passed the forts almost unscathed.

Note 10. (Page 33.)

Just as the Tennessee made for the fort, her ensign was shot away, creating the impression among the Unionists that she had surrendered, and great was their disappointment when they saw it go up again.

Note 11. (Page 34.)

When Farragut made signal *Gunboats chase enemy's gunboats*, Jouett was off in a moment. His vessel was very fast, but, owing to the fact that she drew much more water than the Confederate gunboats, he found himself, before long, *dragging the bottom*. The executive officer, Lieutenant Sleeper, than whom no cooler man lived, reported to him that the Metacomet had *a foot less water under her bottom than her draught*. This was startling; for, should the vessel ground hard, the pursued might return upon the pursuer, and change the game somewhat. "Call the leadsmen in from the chains, Mr. Sleeper!" ordered Jouett. Mr. Sleeper looked amazed. "I tell you," said Jouett, who idolized Farragut, and was a strict constructionist, "the admiral has directed me to follow those gunboats, and I am going to do it. Call the men in from the chains at once, sir; they are *demoralizing* me!" At this the crew, who knew their commander well, set up a loud laugh, and the Metacomet continued in pursuit, with the result we know.

Note 12. (Page 34.)

While the gallantry of Buchanan's attack upon the Union fleet must be acknowledged, it was certainly most Quixotic to make it. "*C'est magnifique*," said an old French officer who witnessed the charge of "The Five Hundred," "*mais ce n'est pas la guerre.*"

Note 13. (Page 37.)

The shot which gave the *coup de grace* to the Tennessee was that which destroyed her steering-gear. The credit of firing it has been claimed for several vessels, and there is no *positive* evidence regarding it; but the general opinion of those who were actors in the strife confers the honor upon the Chickasaw; and the verdict is justified, I think, by the report of the board of officers who held a "strict and careful survey" upon the ram, a few days after the action. The difficulty of establishing a matter of this kind beyond cavil is shown in the fact that several of our commanders lay claim to the honor of *shooting away* the Tennessee's smoke-stack, while Captain Johnston says (page 76): "At about the same time, the smoke-pipe, which had been riddled by shot, was broken close off to the top of the shield, or upper deck, *by the concussion produced by the ramming process adopted by the heavy vessels of the enemy*," &c., &c.

Note 14. (Page 37.)

As the opinion has been very generally expressed, that Buchanan should have made his attack on the Union fleet after nightfall, the following extract from a little memorandum-book, carried by Farragut in his pocket on that memorable 5th of August, is of great interest, as showing that *our* admiral was prepared for every emergency: "Had Buchanan remained under the fort, I should have attacked him as soon as it became so dark as to prevent Page, amid the smoke of our guns, from distinguishing friend from foe. I intended to go in with the three monitors — myself on board the Manhattan."

Note 15. (Page 39.)

It will be observed that General Maury, in his official reports, expresses great indignation at the "precipitate" evacuation of Fort Powell, and the surrender of Fort Gaines; yet it appears more than probable that, in the light of after experience, this distinguished officer's views must have been materially modified.

As to Lieutenant-Colonel Williams, there can be no doubt that he acted wisely and prudently; for, had he remained in Fort Powell, the monitors Chickasaw and Winnebago, and the light-draught gunboats moving up, on August 6th, to within a few hundred yards of its eastern face, and crossing their fire with De Kraft's flotilla outside, would have forced a surrender in less than twelve hours, and the garrison, which Williams saved for the defence of Mobile, have fallen into our hands.

With regard to forts Morgan and Gaines, the question seems to be one purely of time. If there had been a Confederate *army* marching to the relief of Mobile, it would undoubtedly have been the duty of General Page and Colonel Anderson to hold their forts to the last extremity; but so far was this from being the case, that General Maury, according to his own statement, was at that very time sending reinforcements to co-operate with Forrest in holding in check "a force of fifteen thousand men advancing down the Mississippi Central road," while only one thousand "reserves" could be mustered to aid the scanty garrison of four thousand soldiers, citizens, and militia manning the works about Mobile. Remembering, then, that Fort Morgan held out only one day after it was fully invested, the thoughtful reader cannot fail to be impressed with the idea that General Page would have done well had he blown up Fort Morgan as soon as the Union fleet was in undisputed possession of Mobile Bay, and marched his troops to Mobile; and that Colonel Anderson's duty to his soldiers, *many of whom were mere boys*, required him to act, under the circumstances, precisely as he did.

Note 16. (Page 44.)

The following *trova* of Mossen Jaime Febrer, an Arragonese troubadour of the thirteenth century, will doubtless be of interest to many readers, since it relates to Don Pedro Ferragut, one of the "conquerors" of Majorca, from whom *our* Farragut is said to have descended.

PEDRO FERRAGUT.

Troba 237.

Sobre camp bermell una ferradura
De finisim or, ab un clav daurat,
Pere Ferragut pinta, é en tal figura
Esplica lo agnom. La historia asegura
Ser aragones, de Jaca baixat.
Apres que en Mallorca servi de sargent,
Venint á Valencia, hon gran renom guanya
De expert capitá per lo dilitgent;
Los anys, é succesos lo feven prudent
Té en lo pelear gran cordura é manya,
Perque á totes armes fácilment se apanya.

The above may be rendered into English thus: Peter Ferragut, in order that all might know his agnomen, painted upon the vermilion of his shield a golden nail and horse-shoe.

History informs us that he was born in Jaca, in Aragon. After serving as a sergeant in Mallorca, he went to Valencia, where he gained great renown as a captain whose age and experience had made him at once adventurous and prudent. He was famous for his skill in the use of arms, *and for his great amiability in battle.*

BATTLE OF MOBILE BAY.

BY COMMODORE THOMAS H. STEVENS, U. S. N.

Fair broke the morn off Mobile Bay;
On Morgan's crest its first beams play;
O'er stately ships, and mirrored deep,
The blushes of the morning creep.

Fair broke the morn; on distant strand
The rippling waters kiss the land;
The spirit of repose rests there,
To greet the morn so bright, so fair.

O, Morn of Peace! no token thou
Of changing scene that greets us now.
Like phantom craft, at given sign,
The stately ships swing into line.

Stately and grand, in dark array,
Slow moves the Fleet for Mobile Bay;
With the first beam of morning sun
Booms o'er the sea the signal gun.

With the first beam of morning sun,
With the first flash of signal gun,
Fierce broke the battle's angry blast,
Through riven hull and shivered mast.

The red-lipped guns their missiles sent
From ships to forts and battlement;
And fiercer, angrier than before,
Like voice of storms, the battle's roar.

Still swells the storm; no line of fire
Stops the stout heart from its desire;
Resistless as the march of Fate,
Slow moves the Fleet to Mobile's Gate.

Slow moves the Fleet: what stops the way,
To bring disaster on the day?
Who dares to deeds of high emprise
Counts not the cost, nor sacrifice!

To these high praise and meed belong
From the celestial sons of song;
Who nobly dares, like Craven strives,
Shall live immortal as the skies.

Dark grew the day; beneath the wave
Bold Craven finds a warrior's grave;
Confused, defenceless, helpless, lay
The Union Fleet near Mobile Bay.

Quickly did foeman's eye discern
The changing tide of battle turn;
On iron ships, on ships of oak,
Anew the scathing tempest broke.

Great souls with the occasion rise,
Inspired by Him who rules the skies;
With faith unshaken, clear eyes see
The means and path to victory.

THE BATTLE OF MOBILE BAY.

Lashed to the mast, our great chief saw
The coming crisis of the war;
Quick to divine, and firm as rock,
His great soul rose to meet the shock.

Then from aloft was heard the cry,
"Forward! Why linger here to die?"
We saw the HARTFORD lead the way —
The ships once more in firm array.

Forward and onward sweeps the Fleet,
By battered forts, fresh foes to meet;
O'er sunken mines, that strew the bay,
Through shot and shell, that round us play.

Like lions, crouching in their lair,
The foemen's ships in wait lie there, —
With raking cannon guard the way,
Where lay our course, up Mobile Bay.

Short, sharp, decisive was the stroke,
As through their serried line we broke;
Victorious, at noon of day,
Anchored our Fleet in Mobile Bay.

APPENDIX.

ATTACK ON THE DEFENCES OF MOBILE.

Detailed Report of Rear-Admiral D. G. Farragut.

United States Flag-Ship Hartford,
Mobile Bay, August 12, 1864.

Sir: I had the honor to forward to the department, on the evening of the 5th instant, a report of my *entrée* into Mobile Bay, on the morning of that day, and which, though brief, contained all the principal facts of the attack.

Notwithstanding the loss of life, particularly on this ship, and the terrible disaster to the Tecumseh, the result of the fight was a glorious victory, and I have reason to feel proud of the officers, seamen, and marines of the squadron under my command, for it has never fallen to the lot of an officer to be thus situated and thus sustained.

Regular discipline will bring men to any amount of endurance, but there is a natural fear of hidden dangers, particularly when so awfully destructive of human life as the torpedo, which requires more than discipline to overcome.

Preliminary to a report of the action of the fifth, I desire to call the attention of the department to the previous steps taken in consultation with Generals Canby and Granger. On the 8th of July I had an interview with these officers on board the Hartford, on the subject of an attack upon forts Morgan and Gaines, at which it was agreed that General Canby would send all the troops he could spare to co-operate with the fleet. Circumstances soon obliged General Canby to inform me that he could not dispatch a sufficient number to invest both forts; and, in reply, I suggested that Gaines should be first invested, engaging to have a force in the sound ready to protect the landing of the army on Dauphine Island, in the rear of that fort, and I assigned Lieutenant-Commander De Kraft, of the Conemaugh, to that duty.

On the 1st instant General Granger visited me again on the Hartford. In the meantime the Tecumseh had arrived at Pensacola, and Captain Craven had informed me that he would be ready in four days for any service. We therefore fixed upon the 4th of August as the day for the landing of the troops and my entrance into the bay, but owing to delays mentioned in Captain Jenkins' communication to me, the Tecumseh was not ready. General Granger, however, to my mortification, was up to time, and the troops actually landed on Dauphine Island.

As subsequent events proved, the delay turned to our advantage, as the rebels were busily engaged during the 4th in throwing troops and supplies into Fort Gaines, all of which were captured a few days afterward.

The Tecumseh arrived on the evening of the 4th, and

everything being propitious, I proceeded to the attack on the following morning.

As mentioned in my previous despatch, the vessels outside the bar, which were designed to participate in the engagement, were all under way by forty minutes past five in the morning, in the following order, two abreast, and lashed together: — Brooklyn, Captain James Alden, with the Octorora, Lieutenant-Commander C. H. Green, on the port side; Hartford, Captain Percival Drayton, with the Metacomet, Lieutenant-Commander J. E. Jouett; Richmond, Captain T. A. Jenkins, with the Port Royal, Lieutenant-Commander B. Gherardi; Lackawanna, Captain J. B. Marchand, with the Seminole, Commander E. Donaldson; Monongahela, Commander J. H. Strong, with the Kennebec, Lieutenant-Commander W. P. McCann; Ossipee, Commander W. E. Le Roy, with the Itasca, Lieutenant-Commander George Brown; Oneida, Commander J. R. M. Mullany, with the Galena, Lieutenant-Commander C. H. Wells. The iron-clads— Tecumseh, Commander T. A. M. Craven; the Manhattan, Commander J. W. A. Nicholson; the Winnebago, Commander T. H. Stevens; and the Chickasaw, Lieutenant-Commander G. H. Perkins— were already inside the bar, and had been ordered to take up their positions on the starboard side of the wooden ships, or between them and Fort Morgan, for the double purpose of keeping down the fire from the water battery and the parapet guns of the fort, as well as to attack the ram Tennessee as soon as the fort was passed.

It was only at the urgent request of the captains and commanding officers that I yielded to the Brooklyn being the leading ship of the line, as she had four chase guns and an ingenious arrangement for picking up torpedoes, and because, in their judgment, the flag-ship ought not to be too much exposed. This I believe to be an error; for, apart from the fact that exposure is one of the penalties of rank in the navy, it will always be the aim of the enemy to destroy the flag-ship, and, as will appear in the sequel, such attempt was very persistently made, but Providence did not permit it to be successful.

The attacking fleet steamed steadily up the main ship-channel, the Tecumseh firing the first shot at forty-seven minutes past six o'clock. At six minutes past seven the fort opened upon us, and was replied to by a gun from the Brooklyn, and immediately after the action became general.

It was soon apparent that there was some difficulty ahead. The Brooklyn, for some cause which I did not then clearly understand, but which has since been explained by Captain Alden in his report, arrested the advance of the whole fleet, while, at the same time, the guns of the fort were playing with great effect upon that vessel and the Hartford. A moment after I saw the Tecumseh, struck by a torpedo, disappear almost instantaneously beneath the waves, carrying with her her gallant commander and nearly all her crew. I determined at once, as I had originally intended, to take the lead; and after ordering the Metacomet to send a boat to save, if possible, any of the perishing crew, I dashed ahead with the Hartford, and the ships followed on, their officers believing that they were going to a noble death with their commander-in-chief.

I steamed through between the buoys, where the torpedoes were supposed to have been sunk. These buoys

APPENDIX. 61

had been previously examined by my flag-lieutenant, J. Crittenden Watson, in several nightly reconnoissances. Though he had not been able to discover the sunken torpedoes, yet we had been assured, by refugees, deserters, and others, of their existence; but believing that, from their having been some time in the water, they were probably innocuous, I determined to take the chance of their explosion.

From the moment I turned to the northward, to clear the middle ground, we were enabled to keep such a broadside fire upon the batteries of Fort Morgan, that their guns did us comparatively little injury.

Just after we passed the fort, which was about ten minutes before eight o'clock, the ram Tennessee dashed out at this ship, as had been expected, and in anticipation of which I had ordered the monitors on our starboard side. I took no further notice of her than to return her fire.

The rebel gunboats Morgan, Gaines, and Selma were ahead; and the latter particularly annoyed us with a raking fire, which our guns could not return. At two minutes after eight o'clock I ordered the Metacomet to cast off and go in pursuit of the Selma. Captain Jouett was after her in a moment, and in an hour's time he had her as a prize. She was commanded by P. V. Murphy, formerly of the United States navy. He was wounded in the wrist, his executive officer, Lieutenant Comstock, and eight of the crew killed, and seven or eight wounded. Lieutenant-Commander Jouett's conduct during the whole affair commands my warmest commendations. The Morgan and Gaines succeeded in escaping under the protection of the guns of Fort Morgan, which would have been prevented had the other gunboats been as prompt in their movements as the Metacomet; the want of pilots, however, I believe, was the principal difficulty. The Gaines was so injured by our fire that she had to be run ashore, where she was subsequently destroyed; but the Morgan escaped to Mobile during the night, though she was chased and fired upon by our cruisers.

Having passed the forts and dispersed the enemy's gunboats, I had ordered most of the vessels to anchor, when I perceived the ram Tennessee standing up for this ship. This was at forty-five minutes past eight. I was not long in comprehending Buchanan's intentions to be the destruction of the flag-ship. The monitors, and such of the wooden vessels as I thought best adapted for the purpose, were immediately ordered to attack the ram, not only with their guns, but bows on at full speed; and then began one of the fiercest naval combats on record.

The Monongahela, Commander Strong, was the first vessel that struck her, and in doing so carried away her own iron prow, together with the cutwater, without apparently doing her adversary much injury. The Lackawanna, Captain Marchand, was the next vessel to strike her, which she did at full speed; but though her stern was cut and crushed to the plank ends for the distance of three feet above the water's edge to five feet below, the only perceptible effect on the ram was to give her a heavy list.

The Hartford was the third vessel which struck her, but, as the Tennessee quickly shifted her helm, the blow was a glancing one, and, as she rasped along our side, we poured our whole port broadside of nine-inch solid shot within ten feet of her casement.

APPENDIX. 63

The monitors worked slowly, but delivered their fire as opportunity offered. The Chickasaw succeeded in getting under her stern, and a fifteen-inch shot from the Manhattan broke through her iron plating and heavy wooden backing, though the missile itself did not enter the vessel.

Immediately after the collision with the flag-ship, I directed Captain Drayton to bear down for the ram again. He was doing so at full speed, when, unfortunately, the Lackawanna ran into the Hartford just forward of the mizzen-mast, cutting her down to within two feet of the water's edge. We soon got clear again, however, and were fast approaching our adversary, when she struck her colors and ran up the white flag.

She was at this time sore beset; the Chickasaw was pounding away at her stern, the Ossipee was approaching her at full speed, and the Monongahela, Lackawanna, and this ship were bearing down upon her, determined upon her destruction. Her smoke-stack had been shot away, her steering chains were gone, compelling a resort to her relieving tackles, and several of her port-shutters were jammed. Indeed, from the time the Hartford struck her until her surrender, she never fired a gun. As the Ossipee, Commander Le Roy, was about to strike her, she hoisted the white flag, and that vessel immediately stopped her engine, though not in time to avoid a glancing blow.

During this contest with the rebel gunboats and the ram Tennessee, and which terminated by her surrender at ten o'clock, we lost many more men than from the fire of the batteries of Fort Morgan.

Admiral Buchanan was wounded in the leg; two or

three of his men were killed, and five or six wounded. Commander Johnston, formerly of the United States navy, was in command of the Tennessee, and came on board the flag-ship to surrender his sword, and that of Admiral Buchanan. The surgeon, Doctor Conrad, came with him, stated the condition of the admiral, and wished to know what was to be done with him. Fleet Surgeon Palmer, who was on board the Hartford during the action, commiserating the sufferings of the wounded, suggested that those of both sides be sent to Pensacola, where they could be properly cared for. I therefore addressed a note to Brigadier-General R. L. Page, commanding Fort Morgan, informing him that Admiral Buchanan and others of the Tennessee had been wounded, and desiring to know whether he would permit one of our vessels, under a flag of truce, to convey them, with or without our wounded, to Pensacola, on the understanding that the vessel should take out none but the wounded, and bring nothing back that she did not take out. This was acceded to by General Page, and the Metacomet proceeded on this mission of humanity.

I inclose herewith the correspondence with that officer (marked numbers one, two, three, and four.) I forward also the reports (marked numbers five, six, seven, eight, nine, ten, eleven, twelve, thirteen, fourteen, fifteen, sixteen, seventeen, eighteen, nineteen, twenty, and twenty-one) of the commanding officers of the vessels who participated in the action, and who will no doubt call attention to the conduct of such individuals as most distinguished themselves.

As I had an elevated position in the main rigging near the top, I was able to overlook not only the deck of the

Hartford, but the other vessels of the fleet. I witnessed the terrible effects of the enemy's shot, and the good conduct of the men at their guns, and although no doubt their hearts sickened, as mine did, when their shipmates were struck down beside them, yet there was not a moment's hesitation to lay their comrades aside, and spring again to their deadly work.

Our little consort, the Metacomet, was also under my immediate eye during the whole action up to the moment I ordered her to cast off in pursuit of the Selma. The coolness and promptness of Lieutenant-Commander Jouett throughout merit high praise; his whole conduct was worthy of his reputation.

In this connection I must not omit to call the attention of the department to the conduct of Acting Ensign Henry C. Nields, of the Metacomet, who had charge of the boat sent from that vessel when the Tecumseh sank. He took her in under one of the most galling fires I ever saw, and succeeded in rescuing from death ten of her crew, within six hundred yards of the fort. I would respectfully recommend his advancement.

The commanding officers of all the vessels who took part in the action deserve my warmest commendations, not only for the untiring zeal with which they had prepared their ships for the contest, but for their skill and daring in carrying out my orders during the engagement. With the exception of the momentary arrest of the fleet when the Hartford passed ahead, and to which I have already adverted, the order of battle was preserved, and the ships followed each other in close order past the batteries of Fort Morgan, and in comparative safety too, with the exception of the Oneida. Her boilers were penetrated by a shot from the fort, which completely disabled her; but her consort, the Galena, firmly fastened to her side, brought her safely through, showing clearly the wisdom of the precaution of carrying the vessels in two abreast. Commander Mullany, who had solicited eagerly to take part in the action, was severely wounded, losing his left arm.

In the encounter with the ram the commanding officers obeyed with alacrity the order to run her down, and without hesitation exposed their ships to destruction to destroy the enemy.

Our iron-clads, from their slow speed and bad steering, had some difficulty in getting into and maintaining their position in line as we passed the fort, and, in the subsequent encounter with the Tennessee, from the same causes were not as effective as could have been desired; but I cannot give too much praise to Lieutenant-Commander Perkins, who, though he had orders from the department to return north, volunteered to take command of the Chickasaw, and did his duty nobly.

The Winnebago was commanded by Commander T. H. Stevens, who volunteered for that position. His vessel steers very badly, and neither of his turrets will work, which compelled him to turn his vessel every time to get a shot, so that he could not fire very often, but he did the best he could under the circumstances.

The Manhattan appeared to work well, though she moved slowly. Commander Nicholson delivered his fire deliberately, and, as before stated, with one of his fifteen-inch shot broke through the armor of the Tennessee, with its wooden backing, though the shot itself did not enter the vessel. No other shot broke through the armor, though many of her plates were started, and several of her port-shutters jammed by the fire from the different ships.

The Hartford, my flag-ship, was commanded by Captain Percival Drayton, who exhibited throughout that coolness and ability for which he has been long known to his brother officers. But I must speak of that officer in a double capacity. He is the fleet-captain of my squadron, and one of more determined energy, untiring devotion to duty, and zeal for the service, tempered by great calmness, I do not think adorns any navy. I desire to call your attention to this officer, though well aware that in thus speaking of his high qualities, I am only communicating officially to the department that which it knew full well before. To him, and to my staff in their respective positions, I am indebted for the detail of my fleet.

Lieutenant J. Crittenden Watson, my flag-lieutenant, has been brought to your notice in former despatches. During the action he was on the poop attending to the signals, and performed his duties, as might be expected, thoroughly. He is a scion worthy the noble stock he sprang from, and I commend him to your attention.

My secretary, Mr. McKinley, and Acting Ensign H. H. Brownell, were also on the poop, the latter taking notes of the action, a duty which he performed with coolness and accuracy.

Two other acting ensigns of my staff, Mr. Bogart and Mr. Heginbotham, were on duty in the powder division, and, as the reports will show, exhibited zeal and ability. The latter, I regret to add, was severely wounded by a raking shot from the Tennessee when we collided with that vessel, and died a few hours after. Mr. Heginbotham was a young married man, and has left a widow and one child, whom I commend to the kindness of the department.

Lieutenant A. R. Yates, of the Augusta, acted as an additional aid to me on board the Hartford, and was very efficient in the transmission of orders. I have given him the command temporarily of the captured steamer Selma.

The last of my staff, and to whom I would call the attention of the department, is not the least in importance. I mean Pilot Martin Freeman. He has been my great reliance in all difficulties in his line of duty. During the action he was in the main-top, piloting the ships into the bay. He was cool and brave throughout, never losing his self-possession. This man was captured early in the war in a fine fishing-smack which he owned, and though he protested that he had no interest in the war, and only asked for the privilege of fishing for the fleet, yet his services were too valuable to the captors as a pilot not to be secured. He was appointed a first-class pilot, and has served us with zeal and fidelity, and has lost his vessel, which went to pieces on Ship Island. I commend him to the department.

It gives me pleasure to refer to several officers who volunteered to take any situation where they might be useful, some of whom were on their way north, either by orders of the department or condemned by medical survey. The reports of the different commanders will show how they conducted themselves. I have already mentioned Lieutenant-Commander Perkins, of the Chickasaw, and Lieutenant Yates, of the Augusta. Acting

Volunteer Lieutenant William Hamilton, late commanding officer of the Augusta Dinsmore, had been invalided by medical survey, but he eagerly offered his services on board the iron-clad Chickasaw, having had much experience in our monitors. Acting Volunteer Lieutenant P. Giraud, another experienced officer in iron-clads, asked to go in on one of these vessels, but as they were all well supplied with officers, I permitted him to go in on the Ossipee, under Commander Le Roy. After the action he was given temporary charge of the ram Tennessee.

Before closing this report, there is one other officer of my squadron of whom I feel bound to speak, — Captain T. A. Jenkins, of the Richmond, who was formerly my chief of staff, not because of his having held that position, but because he never forgets to do his duty to the government, and takes now the same interest in the fleet as when he stood in that relation to me. He is also the commanding officer of the second division of my squadron, and, as such, has shown ability and the most untiring zeal. He carries out the spirit of one of Lord Collingwood's best sayings: "Not to be afraid of doing too much; those who are, seldom do as much as they ought." When in Pensacola, he spent days on the bar, placing the buoys in the best position, was always looking after the interests of the service, and keeping the vessels from being detained one moment longer in port than was necessary. The gallant Craven told me, only the night before the action in which he lost his life: "I regret, admiral, that I have detained you; but had it not been for Captain Jenkins, God knows when I should have been here. When your order came, I had not received an ounce of coal."

I feel I should not be doing my duty did I not call the attention of the department to an officer who has performed all his various duties with so much zeal and fidelity.

Very respectfully, your obedient servant,

D. G. FARRAGUT,
Commanding W. G. Blockading Squadron.

Hon. Gideon Welles,
Secretary of the Navy.

THE NAVAL FIGHT IN MOBILE BAY.

August 5, 1864.

Official Report of Admiral Buchanan.

United States Naval Hospital, Pensacola,
August 26, 1864.

Sir: I have the honor to inform you that the enemy's fleet, under Admiral Farragut, consisting of fourteen steamers and four monitors, passed Fort Morgan on the 5th instant, about 6.30 A. M., in the following order, and stood into Mobile Bay: — The four monitors, Tecumseh and Manhattan, each carrying two fifteen-inch guns, the Winnebago and Chickasaw, each carrying four eleven-inch guns, in a single line ahead, about half a mile from the fort. The fourteen steamers, — Brooklyn, of twenty-six; Octorora, ten; Hartford, twenty-eight; Metacomet, ten; Richmond, twenty-four; Port Royal, eight; Lackawanna, fourteen; Seminole, nine; Monongahela, twelve; Kennebec, five; Ossipee, thirteen; Itasca, four; Oneida, ten; and Galena, fourteen guns, — in a double line ahead, each two lashed together, the side-wheel steamers off shore, all about one-quarter of a mile from the monitors, — carrying in all one hundred and ninety-nine guns and twenty-seven hundred men. When they were discovered standing into the channel, signal was made to the Mobile squadron, under my command, consisting of the wooden gunboats Morgan and Gaines, each carrying six guns, and Selma, four, to "follow my motions" in the ram Tennessee, of six guns, — in all twenty-two guns, and four hundred and seventy men. All were soon under way, and stood towards the enemy in a line abreast. As the Tennessee approached the fleet, when opposite the fort, we opened our battery at short range upon the leading ship, the admiral's flag-ship Hartford, and made the attempt to run into her, but, owing to her superior speed, our attempt was frustrated. We then stood towards the next heavy ship, the Brooklyn, with the same view; she also avoided us by her superior speed. During this time the gunboats were also closely engaged with the enemy. All our guns were used to the greatest advantage, and we succeeded in seriously damaging many of the enemy's vessels.

The Selma and Gaines, under Lieutenant-Commandants P. U. Murphy and J. W. Bennett, fought gallantly, and I was gratified to hear from officers of the enemy's fleet that their fire was very destructive. The Gaines was fought until she was found to be in a sinking condition, when she was run on shore near Fort Morgan.

Lieutenant-Commandant Murphy was closely engaged with the Metacomet, assisted by the Morgan, Commander G. W. Harrison, who during the conflict deserted him, when, upon the approach of another large steamer, the Selma surrendered. I refer you to the report of Lieutenant-Commandant Murphy for the particulars of his action; he lost two promising young officers, Lieutenant Comstock and Master's Mate Murray, and a number of his men were killed and wounded, and he was also wounded severely in the wrist.* Commander Harrison will no doubt report to the department his reason for leaving the Selma in that contest with the enemy, as the Morgan was uninjured; his conduct is severely commented on by the officers of the enemy's fleet, much to the injury of that officer and the navy. Soon after the gunboats were dispersed by the overwhelming superiority of force, and the enemy's fleet had anchored about four miles above Fort Morgan, we stood for them again, in the Tennessee, and renewed the attack, with the hope of sinking some of them with our prow; again we were foiled by their superior speed in avoiding us. The engagement with the whole fleet soon became general at very close quarters, and lasted about an hour; and, notwithstanding the serious injury inflicted upon many of their vessels by our guns, we could not sink them. Frequently during the contest we were surrounded by the enemy, and all our guns were in action almost at the same moment.

Four of the heaviest vessels ran into us under full steam, with the view of sinking us. One vessel, the Monongahela, had been prepared as a ram, and was very formidable; she struck us with great force, injuring us but little; her prow and stem were knocked off, and the vessel was so much injured as to make it necessary to dock her. Several of the other vessels of the fleet were found to require extensive repairs. I enclose you a copy of a drawing of the Brooklyn, made by one of her officers after the action, and an officer of the Hartford informed me that she was more seriously injured than the Brooklyn.

* A Court of Inquiry exonerated Commander Harrison from blame in this affair. F. A. P.

I mention these facts to prove that the guns of the Tennessee were not idle during this unequal contest. For other details of the action, and injuries sustained by the Tennessee, I refer you to the report of Commander J. D. Johnston, which has my approval. After I was carried below, unfortunately wounded, I had to be governed by the reports of that valuable officer as to the condition of the ship, and the necessity and time of her surrender; and when he represented to me her utterly hopeless condition to continue the fight with injury to the enemy, and suggested her surrender, I directed him to do the best he could, and when he could no longer damage the enemy, to do so.

It affords me much pleasure to state that the officers and men cheerfully fought their guns to the best of their abilities, and gave strong evidence, by their promptness in executing orders, of their willingness to continue the contest as long as they could stand to their guns, notwithstanding the fatigue they had undergone for several hours; and it was only because the circumstances were as represented by Captain Johnston, that she was surrendered to the fleet about ten A. M., painful as it was to do so. I seriously felt the want of experienced officers during the action; all were young and inexperienced, and many had but little familiarity with naval duties, having been appointed from civil life within the year.

The reports of Commander Harrison, of the Morgan, and Lieutenant-Commandant Bennett, of the Gaines, you have, no doubt, received from these officers. I enclose the report of Fleet-Surgeon D. B. Conrad, to whom I am much indebted for his skill, promptness, and attention to the wounded. By permission of Admiral Farragut, he accompanied the wounded of the Tennessee and Selma to this hospital, and is assisted by Assistant-Surgeons Booth and Bowles of the Selma and Tennessee, all under the charge of Fleet-Surgeon Palmer, of the United States navy, from whom we have received all the attention and consideration we could desire or expect.

The crews, and many officers of the Tennessee and Selma, have been sent to New Orleans. Commander J. D. Johnston, Lieutenant-Commandant P. U. Murphy, Lieutenants W. L. Bradford and A. D. Wharton, Second Assistant Engineer J. C. O'Connell, and myself, are to be sent north. Master's Mates, W. S. Forrest and R. M. Carter, who are with me acting as my aids, not having any midshipmen, are permitted to accompany me. They are valuable young officers, zealous in their duties, and both have served in the army, where they received honorable wounds; their services are important to me. I am happy to inform you that my wound is improving, and I sincerely hope our exchange will be effected, and that I will soon again be on duty.

Enclosed is a list of the officers of the Tennessee who were in the action.

September 17th. Since writing the above, I have seen the report of Admiral Farragut, a portion of which is incorrect. Captain Johnston did not deliver my sword on board the Hartford. After the surrender of the Tennessee, Captain Giraud, the officer who was sent on board to take charge of her, said to me that he was directed by Admiral Farragut to ask for my sword, which was brought from the cabin and delivered to him by one of my aids.

ADMIRAL F. BUCHANAN, *commanding.*

EXTRACT

FROM A LETTER OF COMMANDER J. D. JOHNSTON TO THE EDITOR OF THE "PLANTATION," AUGUST 5, 1871.

"The steering apparatus of the ship was defective from the first, and it seemed almost impracticable to protect it against the inevitable destruction which awaited it in such an engagement. The enemy having discovered, when running into the ship, that the chains leading to the rudder-head were exposed on the after-deck, turned his attention especially to their destruction, which was of course easily effected at such close quarters. At about the same time, the smoke-pipe, which had been riddled by shot, was broken close off to the top of the shield, or upper deck, by the concussion produced by the ramming process adopted by the heavy vessels of the enemy, and the smoke and heat issuing from the broken pipe came down upon the men at the guns with almost insupportable effect.

"The ports of the ship were covered when the guns were run in for loading, by heavy iron covers, which revolved on pivots; but it unfortunately happened that those of the bow and stern ports were so jammed against the side of the shield by the enemy's shot, that it became impossible to move them, and it was while superintending a mechanic who was endeavoring to back out one of these pivot bolts, so as to bring the stern gun into action again,

APPENDIX. 77

that Admiral Buchanan received a wound in his leg, which disabled him completely. The poor machinist was crushed by the same shot so that his remains had the appearance of sausage meat, and one of the gun's crew was also killed by an iron splinter. After the wheel chains leading to the rudder-head were destroyed, the 'relieving tackles' were used to steer the ship, but she was not long permitted to avail herself of this expedient, a shot having taken away blocks and tackle both, only a few moments after they were resorted to."

REPORT.

CASUALTIES IN THE UNION FLEET, IN THE ATTACK ON THE DEFENCES OF MOBILE HARBOR.

Report of Rear-Admiral D. G. Farragut.

FLAG-SHIP HARTFORD, MOBILE BAY,
August 8, 1864.

SIR: In my despatch, number three hundred and thirty-five, written on the evening of the engagement of the 5th instant, the casualties then reported were forty-one killed, and eighty-eight wounded.

More detailed reports, since received, make the casualties fifty-two killed, and one hundred and seventy wounded, namely:

	Killed.	Wounded.
Hartford,	25	28
Brooklyn,	11	43

	Killed.	Wounded.
Lackawanna,	4	35
Oneida,	8	30
Monongahela,	0	6
Metacomet,	1	2
Ossipee,	1	7
Richmond,	0	2 slightly.
Galena,	0	1
Octorora,	1	10
Kennebec,	1	6

I forward herewith the reports of the surgeons of these vessels, giving the names of the killed and wounded, and the character of the wounds.

Very respectfully, your obedient servant,

D. G. FARRAGUT,
Rear-Admiral, commanding W. G. B. Squadron.

HON. GIDEON WELLES, *Secretary of the Navy,*
Washington.

KILLED AND WOUNDED OF CONFEDERATE FLEET, IN ACTION OF AUGUST 5, 1864, MOBILE BAY.

"TENNESSEE," FLAG-SHIP.

Killed.— John Silk, first-class fireman; William Moors, seaman. — 2.

Wounded.— Admiral F. Buchanan, fracture right leg; A. T. Post, pilot, slightly in head; J. C. O'Connell, second assistant engineer, slightly in leg and shoulder; William Rogers, second assistant engineer, slightly in head and shoulder; James Kelly, B. M., slightly in knee; And. Rasmison, Q. M., slightly in head; William Daly, seaman, in head; Robert Barry, marine, gunshot wound of ear and head; James McKunn, marine, contusion of shoulder. — 9.

"SELMA." P. U. MURPHY, *Lieutenant commanding.*

Killed.— J. H. Comstock, lieutenant, and executive officer; J. R. Murray, acting master's mate; William Hall, gunner's mate; James Rooney, seaman; James Montgomery, seaman; Bernard Riley, ordinary seaman; J. R. Frisly, landsman; Christopher Shepard, landsman. — 8.

Wounded.— P. U. Murphy, lieutenant, commanding, slightly in wrist; John Villa, seaman, badly, leg and arm; Henry Fratee, landsman, badly in hand; Daniel Linnehan, seaman, slightly in arm; John Shick, seaman, slightly in face; John Davis, fireman, slightly; John Gilliland, seaman, slightly. — 7.

Total — killed, 10; wounded, 16.

D. B. CONRAD,
Fleet Surgeon, C. S. N.

OFFICERS OF THE CONFEDERATE RAM "TENNESSEE."

Admiral, F. Buchanan, *Commander-in-Chief*.
Commander, J. D. Johnston.
First Lieutenant, Wm. L. Bradford, (executive officer.)
Lieutenants, A. D. Wharton, E. J. McDermett.

Masters, H. W. Perrin, J. Demaley.

Master's Mates, M. J. Beebe, R. M. Carter, and W. S. Forrest.

Boatswain, John McCradie.

Gunner, H. S. Smith.

First Lieutenant Marines, D. G. Raney.

First Assistant Engineer, G. D. Lening.

Second Assistant Engineers, J. C. O'Connell, and John Hays.

Third Assistant Engineers, William Rogers, Oscar Benson, and William Patterson.

Fleet-Surgeon, D. B. Conrad.

Assistant-Surgeon, R. C. Bowles.

OFFICERS OF THE UNION SHIPS WHICH PASSED THE FORTS, AND WERE ENGAGED WITH THE CONFEDERATE RAM AND GUNBOATS.

"HARTFORD."

Rear-Admiral, David Glasgow Farragut, *Commander-in-Chief*.

Fleet Captain, Percival Drayton.

Lieutenant-Commander, Lewis A. Kimberly, (executive officer.)

Lieutenants, J. Crittenden Watson, A. R. Yates, Herbert B. Tyson, and La Rue P. Adams.

Acting Volunteer Lieutenant, George Mundy.

Acting Ensigns, G. D. B. Glidden, William H. Whiting, H. H. Brownell, H. H. Heginbotham, Robert D. Bogart, and William L. Dana.

Acting Master's Mates, Richard P. Herrick, George B. Avery, William H. Hathorne, William H. Childs, and Joseph J. Finelli.

Captain Marines, Charles Heywood.

Rear-Admiral's Secretary, Alexander McKinley.

Fleet Engineer, William H. Shock.

Chief Engineer, Thomas Williamson.

First Assistant Engineer, Edward B. Latch.

Second Assistant Engineers, John Wilson, Isaac De Graff, and H. L. Pelkington.

Third Assistant Engineer, James E. Speights.

Acting Third Assistant Engineers, William McEwan, T. Benton Brown, and John D. Thompson.

Fleet Surgeon, J. C. Palmer.

Surgeon, Philip Lansdale.

Assistant Surgeons, William Commons, and F. Woolverton.

Fleet Paymaster, Edward T. Dunn.

Paymaster, William F. Meredith.

"BROOKLYN."

Captain, James Alden.

Lieutenant-Commander, Edward P. Lull, (executive officer.)

Lieutenants, Thomas L. Swann, and Charles F. Blake.

Ensigns, Charles H. Pendleton, and C. D. Sigsbee.

Acting Ensigns, John Atter, and D. R. Cassel.

Acting Master's Mates, Frederick C. Duncan, A. L. Stevens, and William H. Cook.

Chief Engineer, Mortimer Kellogg.

Second Assistant Engineers, John D. Toppin, David Hardie, Haviland Barstow, and George E. Tower.

Third Assistant Engineers, F. C. Goodwin, Joel A. Bullard, and William H. De Hart.

Acting Third Assistant Engineer, Henry H. Arthur.

Surgeon, George Maulsby.

Assistant Surgeon, H. Smith.

Paymaster, Gilbert E. Thornton.

"RICHMOND."

Captain, Thornton A. Jenkins.

Lieutenant-Commander, Edward Terry, (executive officer.)

Acting Volunteer Lieutenant, Charles J. Gibbs.

Acting Master, Prince S. Borden.

Ensign, Philip H. Cooper.

Acting Ensigns, Lewis Clark, Colby M. Chester, and Arthur H. Wright.

Acting Master's Mates, James West, Theodore J. Werner, William C. Seymour, and Walter A. De Witt.

Second Lieutenant Marines, C. L. Sherman.

Chief Engineer, Jackson McElmell.

First Assistant Engineer, Emory J. Brooks.

Second Assistant Engineers, Albert J. Kenyon, Absalom Kirby, John D. Ford, and Robert Weir.

Third Assistant Engineers, William H. Crawford, Charles W. C. Sartar, James W. Patterson, and Thomas McElmell.

Surgeon, Lewis J. Williams.

Assistant Surgeon, J. McD. Rice.

Paymaster, Edwin Stewart.

"LACKAWANNA."

Captain, J. B. Marchand.
Lieutenants, Thomas S. Spencer, (executive officer,) S. A. McCarty.
Acting Masters, Felix McCurley, and John H. Allen.
Ensigns, G. H. Wadleigh, and Frank Wildes.
Acting Ensign, Clarence Rathbone.
Acting Master's Mates, William J. Lewis, C. H. Foster, and John C. Palmer.
First Assistant Engineer, James W. Whittaker.
Second Assistant Engineers, E. J. Whittaker, and George W. Roche.
Third Assistant Engineer, Isaac B. Fort.
Acting Third Assistant Engineers, David F. Hennessy, and George W. Sullivan.
Surgeon, T. W. Leach.
Acting Assistant Surgeon, W. T. Hutchinson.
Paymaster, James Fulton.

"MONONGAHELA."

Commander, James H. Strong.
Lieutenants, Roderick Prentiss, (executive officer,) O. A. Batcheller.
Acting Ensigns, D. W. Mullan, James H. Rodgers, George Gerard, and P. E. Harrington.
Chief Engineer, George E. Kutz.
Second Assistant Engineers, Joseph Trilly, J. J. Bissett, Edward Cheeney, and Philip J. Sanger.
Acting Third Assistant Engineer, Amos C. Wilcox.
Surgeon, David Kindleberger.
Acting Assistant Surgeon, William B. Lewis.
Assistant Paymaster, Forbes Parker.

"OSSIPEE."

Commander, William E. Le Roy.
Lieutenants, J. A. Howell, (executive officer,) Richard S. Chew.
Acting Masters, C. C. Bunker, and C. W. Adams.
Acting Ensigns, Charles E. Clark, Henry S. Lambert, and William A. Van Vleck.
Acting Master's Mates, George Pilling, and William Merrigood.
Acting Chief Engineer, James M. Adams.
Second Assistant Engineer, William H. Vanderbilt.
Acting Second Assistant Engineers, Martin H. Gerry, James R. Webb, George W. Kidder, and Alfred Colin.
Third Assistant Engineer, John Matthews.
Acting Third Assistant Engineer, William Collier.
Surgeon, B. F. Gibbs.
Acting Assistant Surgeon, John K. Bacon.
Paymaster, Edward Foster.

"ONEIDA."

Commander, J. R. Madison Mullany.
Lieutenant, Charles L. Huntington, (executive officer.)
Lieutenants, Charles S. Cotton, and Edward N. Kellogg.
Ensign, Charles V. Gridley.
Acting Ensigns, John L. Hall, and John Sears.
Acting Master's Mates, Edward Bird, Daniel Clark, and John Devereaux.
Chief Engineer, William H. Hunt.

First Assistant Engineer, Reuben H. Fitch.
Acting Third Assistant Engineers, W. E. Deaver, and Nicholas Dillon.
Surgeon, John Y. Taylor.
Acting Paymaster, George R. Martin.

"METACOMET."

Lieutenant-Commander, James E. Jouett.
Acting Volunteer Lieutenant, Henry J. Sleeper, (executive officer.)
Acting Masters, N. M. Dyer, and John O. Morse.
Acting Ensigns, George E. Wing, John White, and Henry C. Nields.
Acting Master's Mates, J. K. Goodwin, and Rufus N. Miller.
First Assistant Engineer, James Atkins.
Second Assistant Engineer, George P. Hunt.
Third Assistant Engineers, George B. Rodgers, James H. Nash, and D. W. King.
Acting Assistant Surgeon, E. D. Payne.
Acting Assistant Paymaster, H. M. Hamman.

"OCTORORA."

Lieutenant-Commander, Charles H. Greene.
Acting Volunteer Lieutenant, William D. Urann, (executive officer.)
Acting Masters, H. S. Young, and Henry R. Billings.
Acting Ensign, George H. Dodge.

Acting Master's Mates, George P. Gifford, and George W. Adams.

Acting First Assistant Engineers, William W. Shipman, and M. N. McEntee.

Second Assistant Engineer, Rozeau B. Plotts.

Acting Second Assistant Engineer, Jarol Huber.

Acting Third Assistant Engineers, Joseph Knight, and Gustav W. Best.

Assistant Surgeon, Edward R. Dodge.

Acting Assistant Paymaster, Joseph H. Pynchon.

"PORT ROYAL."

Lieutenant-Commander, Bancroft Gherardi.

Lieutenant-Commander, Thomas C. Bowen, (executive officer.)

Acting Masters, Edward Herrick, and Thomas M. Gardner.

Acting Ensigns, William Hull, and Fortesque S. Hopkins.

Acting Master's Mates, Eugene V. Tyson, Henry D. Baldwin, William A. Prescott, and Samuel S. Bumpus.

Acting First Assistant Engineer, Fletcher A. Wilson.

Second Assistant Engineers, Francis B. Allen, and Henry Snyder.

Acting Second Assistant Engineer, John B. McGavern.

Third Assistant Engineer, W. C. F. Reichenbuck.

Acting Assistant Surgeon, Edward R. Hutchins.

Acting Assistant Paymaster, Frank K. Moore.

"SEMINOLE."

Commander, Edward Donaldson.
Acting Volunteer Lieutenant, John A. Johnston, (executive officer.)
Acting Master, William A. Marine.
Acting Ensigns, Francis Kempton, Walter S. Church, and David K. Perkins.
Acting Master's Mates, C. A. Thorne, and Henry Webb.
Acting First Assistant Engineers, Claude Babcock, and Alvin R. Calden.
Acting Third Assistant Engineers, William Drinkwater, Patrick I. Hughes, and William H. Whiting.
Surgeon, John I. Gibson.
Paymaster, Levi J. Stockwell.

"KENNEBEC."

Lieutenant-Commander, William P. McCann.
Acting Volunteer Lieutenant, Edward Baker, (executive officer.)
Acting Ensigns, John J. Butler, Hosea E. Tinkham, and Joseph D. Ellis.
Second Assistant Engineers, Lewis W. Robinson, and John S. Pearce.
Acting Third Assistant Engineer, James Eccles.
Acting Assistant Surgeon, George W. Hatch.
Acting Assistant Paymaster, Edward T. Baker.

"ITASCA."

Lieutenant-Commander, George Brown.
Acting Master, Richard Eustace, (executive officer.)
Acting Ensigns, Charles H. Hurd, James Igo, and Edward S. Lowe.
Acting Master's Mates, L. E. Heath, and Marcus Chapman.
Second Assistant Engineers, John Bothwick, and George C. Irelan.
Acting Third Assistant Engineers, Charles A. Laws, and Alfred Hoyt.
Acting Assistant Surgeon, Henry Brockwood.
Acting Assistant Paymaster, Alfred G. Lathrop.

"GALENA."

Lieutenant-Commander, Clark H. Wells.
Acting Volunteer Lieutenant, Charles H. Wilson, (executive officer.)
Acting Master, D. W. C. Kells.
Acting Ensigns, Henry Pease, Jr., and Sanford S. Miner.
Acting Master's Mates, Francis Tuttle, and James H. Delano.
First Assistant Engineer, William G. Buchler.
Second Assistant Engineers, Charles H. Greenleaf, and John A. Scot.
Acting Third Assistant Engineers, Patrick Burns, and William Welcker.
Acting Assistant Surgeon, George P. Wright.
Acting Assistant Paymaster, Theodore Kitchen.

"Tecumseh."

Commander, T. Augustus Craven.
Lieutenant, John W. Kelly, (executive officer.)
Acting Masters, Charles F. Langley, and Gardner Cottrell.
Acting Ensigns, John P. Lettic, and William Titcomb.
Chief Engineer, C. Faron.
Second Assistant Engineers, F. S. Barlow, and Henry S. Leonard.
Acting Second Assistant Engineer, T. Ustick.
Acting Third Assistant Engineers, George Relter, and James L. Parsons.
Acting Assistant Surgeon, William A. Danker.
Acting Assistant Paymaster, George Worke.

"Manhattan."

Commander, J. W. A. Nicholson.
Lieutenant, E. M. Schoonmaker, (executive officer.)
Acting Master, Robert B. Ely.
Acting Ensigns, John B. Trott, George B. Mott, and Peter France.
Acting Chief Engineer, C. L. Carty.
Acting First Assistant Engineer, William H. Miller.
Acting Second Assistant Engineers, James B. Farrand, and Thomas Finnie.
Acting Third Assistant Engineers, Edward Misset, Charles F. Stroud, and Harrie Webster.
Assistant Surgeon, John H. Austin.
Acting Assistant Paymaster, H. G. Thayer.

"WINNEBAGO."

Commander, Thomas H. Stevens.

Acting Volunteer Lieutenant, William F. Shankland, (executive officer.)

Acting Master, Austrony S. Megathlin.

Acting Ensigns, James Whitworth, Michael Murphy, and John Morrisey.

Acting Master's Mates, Henry C. Atter, John L. Hall, William Edgar, and Charles S. Lyons.

Acting Chief Engineer, Simon Shultice.

First Assistant Engineer, John Purdy.

Acting First Assistant Engineers, James Munroe, and John Wilson.

Acting Second Assistant Engineers, E. L. Morse, and Philip Allman.

Acting Third Assistant Engineers, Robert D. Wright, James W. Quinn, James Morris, and Thomas J. Myers.

Acting Assistant Surgeon, Joseph G. Bell.

Acting Assistant Paymaster, Henry Gerrard.

"CHICKASAW."

Lieutenant-Commander, George H. Perkins.

Acting Volunteer Lieutenant, William Hamilton, (executive officer.)

Acting Masters, Ezekiel D. Percy, and E. B. Pike.

Acting Ensigns, George L. Jorden, and J. Louis Harris.

Acting Master's Mates, Allen A. Mann, M. F. Kershaw, M. G. Jones, and F. A. Case.

Acting Chief Engineer, William Rodgers.

Acting First Assistant Engineer, Charles Chadwick.

Acting Second Assistant Engineers, Elisha P. Bartlett, James J. Maratta, and Thomas H. Nelson.

Acting Third Assistant Engineers, Albert H. Goff, Sarill Whitehead, Alexander H. Wiggins, Alfred Wilkinson, Henry Wentworth, and George Harris.

Acting Assistant Surgeon, Garrett D. Buckner.

Acting Assistant Paymaster, Edmund S. Wheeler.

ROLL OF HONOR.

The following Roll of Honor is taken from "The Record of the Medals of Honor issued to the Blue Jackets and Marines of the Navy, under authority of the Congress of the United States, for Deeds of Gallantry and Heroism in times of War and of Peace."

WILSON BROWN,

Landsman on board of the United States steamer "Hartford," in the engagement in Mobile Bay, August 5, 1864. "Was stationed at the shell-whip on the berth deck. A man was killed on the ladder above him, and thrown with such violence against Brown as to knock him into the hold, where he lay for a short time senseless; but on recovering he immediately returned to his station, though, besides himself, only one of the original six belonging there had escaped."

THOMAS FITZPATRICK,

Coxswain on board of the United States steamer "Hartford," in the engagement in Mobile Bay, August 5, 1864. "His gun was disabled by the bursting of a shell, which destroyed much of the material and killed seven men, besides wounding several others, and among them himself. Notwithstanding this, he had the killed and wounded quietly removed; replaced the breeching, side-tackle and truck, &c. (which had been cut to pieces); got a crew, and in a little while was firing the gun again as usual."

MARTIN FREEMAN,

Pilot on board of the United States steamer "Hartford," in the engagement in Mobile Bay, August 5, 1864. "Was the great reliance of the commanding officer of the 'Hartford,' in all difficulties in his line of duty. During the action he was in the main-top, piloting the ships into the bay. Especially commended to the department."

JAMES R. GARRISON,

Coal-heaver on board of the United States steamer "Hartford," in the engagement in Mobile Bay, August 5, 1864. "Had one of his great toes shot off; but without leaving his station at the shell-whip, bound up the wound, and remained at work until again severely wounded."

JOHN LAWSON,

Landsman on board of the United States steamer "Hartford," in the engagement in Mobile Bay, August 5, 1864. "Was one of the six men stationed at the shell-whip on the berth deck. A shell killed or wounded the whole number. Lawson was wounded in the leg, and thrown with great violence against the side of the ship; but as soon as he recovered himself, although begged to go below, he refused, and went back to the shell-whip, where he remained during the action."

John McFarland,

Captain of forecastle on board of the United States steamer "Hartford," in the engagement in Mobile Bay, August 5, 1864. "Was at the wheel, which has been his station in all of the previous fights of this ship. As on every other occasion, he displayed the utmost coolness and intelligence throughout the action. When the 'Lackawanna' ran into the 'Hartford,' and for a moment there was every appearance of the men at the wheel being crushed, he never left his station, nor ceased for an instant to attend strictly to his duties. This evidence of coolness and self-possession, together with his good conduct in the other battles of the 'Hartford,' entitles him to the medal."

Charles Melville,

Ordinary Seaman on board of the United States steamer "Hartford," in the engagement in Mobile Bay, August 5, 1864. "This man (a loader of the same gun) was severely wounded by a piece of the shell. He was taken below, but would not remain there; and although scarcely able to stand, performed his duty until the end of the action."

Thomas O'Connell,

Coal-heaver on board of the United States steamer "Hartford," in the engagement in Mobile Bay, August 5, 1864. "Although on the sick-list, and quite unwell, he went to his station at the shell-whip, where he remained until his right hand was shot away."

WILLIAM PELHAM,

Landsman on board of the United States steamer "Hartford," in the engagement in Mobile Bay, August 5, 1864. "When the crew of the gun to which he belonged was entirely broken up, owing to the number of its killed and wounded, he assisted in removing the latter below, and then immediately returned, and, without any direction to do so, took his place at the adjoining gun, where a vacancy existed, and continued to perform his duties there most faithfully for the remainder of the action."

WILLIAM A. STANLEY,

Shell-man at No. 8 gun on board of the United States steamer "Hartford," in the engagement in Mobile Bay, August 5, 1864. "Was severely wounded, but refused to go below; and continued to perform his duties, until at length he became so weak from loss of blood as to be unable to stand."

JOHN BROWN,

Captain of forecastle on board of the United States steamer "Brooklyn," in the engagement in Mobile Bay, August 5, 1864. Very conspicuous for bravery, skill, coolness, and activity at his gun.

WILLIAM BLAGEEN.

Ship's Cook on board of the United States steamer "Brooklyn," in the engagement in Mobile Bay, August 5,

1864. Conspicuous for bravery, performing his duty in the powder division, at a point where the ship was riddled very much, and in the immediate vicinity of the shell-whips, which were twice cleared of men by bursting shells.

WILLIAM H. BROWN,

Landsman on board of the United States steamer "Brooklyn," in the engagement in Mobile Bay, August 5, 1864. Conspicuous for bravery, performing his duty in the powder division at a point where the ship was riddled very much, and in the immediate vicinity of the shell-whips, which were twice cleared of men by bursting shells. Was also wounded.

JOHN COOPER,

Coxswain on board of the United States steamer "Brooklyn," in the engagement in Mobile Bay, August 5, 1864. Very conspicuous for bravery, skill, coolness, and activity at his gun.

J. HENRY DENIG,

Sergeant of Marines on board of the United States steamer "Brooklyn," in the engagement in Mobile Bay, August 5, 1864. Conspicuous good conduct at his gun.

RICHARD DENNIS,

Boatswain's Mate on board of the United States steamer "Brooklyn," in the engagement in Mobile Bay, August 5, 1864. Displayed much courage, bravery, and coolness in operating the torpedo-catcher and assisting in working the bow-chaser.

SAMUEL W. DAVIS,

Ordinary Seaman on board of the United States steamer "Brooklyn," in the engagement in Mobile Bay, August 5, 1864. Displayed much courage, bravery, and coolness in acting as a lookout for torpedoes and other obstructions.

MICHAEL HUDSON,

Sergeant of Marines on board of the United States steamer "Brooklyn," in the engagement in Mobile Bay, August 5, 1864. Conspicuous good conduct at his gun.

WILLIAM HALSTEAD,

Coxswain on board of the United States steamer "Brooklyn," in the engagement in Mobile Bay, August 5, 1864. Coolness, bravery, and skill in the working of his gun. His conduct was particularly meritorious.

JOSEPH IRLAM,

Seaman on board of the United States steamer "Brooklyn," in the engagement in Mobile Bay, August 5, 1864. Stationed at the wheel; behaved with great coolness and bravery, sending the other two men who were stationed with him to replace men disabled at the guns.

NICHOLAS IRWIN,

Seaman on board of the United States steamer "Brooklyn," in the engagement in Mobile Bay, August 5, 1864. Very conspicuous for bravery, skill, coolness, and activity at his gun.

John Irving,

Coxswain on board of the United States steamer "Brooklyn," in the engagement in Mobile Bay, August 5, 1864. Very conspicuous for bravery, skill, coolness, and activity at his gun.

Burnett Kenna,

Quartermaster on board of the United States steamer "Brooklyn," in the engagement in Mobile Bay, August 5, 1864. Coolness, bravery, and skill in the working of his gun. His conduct was particularly meritorious.

Alexander Mack,

Captain of Top on board of the United States steamer "Brooklyn," in the engagement in Mobile Bay, August 5, 1864. Activity, zeal, and skill displayed in handling his gun, as well as great courage. He was severely wounded.

William Madden,

Coal-heaver on board of the United States steamer "Brooklyn," in the engagement in Mobile Bay, August 5, 1864. Conspicuous for bravery, performing his duty in the powder division, at a point where the ship was riddled very much, and in the immediate vicinity of the shell-whips, which were twice cleared of men by bursting shells.

James Machon,

Boy, United States steamer "Brooklyn," in the engagement in Mobile Bay, August 5, 1864. Conspicuous for bravery, performing his duty in the powder division, at a point where the ship was riddled very much, and in the immediate vicinity of the shell-whips, which were twice cleared of men by bursting shells.

JAMES MIFFLIN,

Landsman on board of the United States steamer "Brooklyn," in the engagement in Mobile Bay, August 5, 1864. Conspicuous for bravery, performing his duty in the powder division, at a point where the ship was riddled very much, and in the immediate vicinity of the shell-whips, which were twice cleared of men by bursting shells.

WILLIAM NICHOLS,

Quartermaster on board of the United States steamer "Brooklyn," in the engagement in Mobile Bay, August 5, 1864. Perfect coolness and dexterity in handling his gun; always sure of his aim before he would consent to fire.

MILES M. OVIATT,

Corporal of Marines on board of the United States steamer "Brooklyn," in the engagement in Mobile Bay, August 5, 1864. Conspicuous for good conduct at his gun.

EDWARD PRICE,

Coxswain on board of the United States steamer "Brooklyn," in the engagement in Mobile Bay, August 5, 1864. Great coolness and bravery under fire. His gun becoming disabled by the sponge breaking, leaving the head in the gun, he proceeded to clear it by pouring powder into the vent and blowing the sponge-head out.

William M. Smith,

Corporal of Marines on board of the United States steamer "Brooklyn," in the engagement in Mobile Bay, August 5, 1864. Conspicuous for good conduct at his gun.

James E. Sterling,

Coal-heaver on board of the United States steamer "Brooklyn," in the engagement in Mobile Bay, August 5, 1864. Bravery in remaining at his post when wounded, and passing shell until struck down a second time, and completely disabled.

Samuel Todd,

Quartermaster on board of the United States steamer "Brooklyn," in the engagement in Mobile Bay, August 5, 1864. Conspicuous coolness at the commencement and during the action.

Thomas Atkinson,

Yeoman on board of the United States steamer "Richmond," Mobile Bay, August 5, 1864. Commended for coolness and energy in supplying the rifle ammunition, which was under his sole charge in the action in Mobile Bay on the morning and forenoon of August 5, 1864. He was a petty officer on board of the United States frigate "Congress" in 1842-46; was present and assisted in capturing the whole of the Buenos Ayrean fleet by that vessel, off Monte Video; joined the "Richmond" in September, 1860; was in the actions with Fort McRea;

the head of the passes of the Mississippi; forts Jackson and St. Philip; the Chalmettes; the rebel iron-clads and gunboats below New Orleans; Vicksburg; Port Hudson; and at the surrender of New Orleans.

ROBERT BROWN,

Captain of Top on board of the United States steamer "Richmond," Mobile Bay, August 5, 1864. Commended for coolness and good conduct in the action in Mobile Bay, on the morning and forenoon of August 5, 1864. He was on board the "Westfield" in the actions with forts Jackson and St. Philip; the Chalmettes; and present at the surrender of New Orleans; also with the batteries at Vicksburg. Joined the "Richmond" in September, 1863.

CORNELIUS CRONIN,

Chief Quartermaster on board of the United States steamer "Richmond," Mobile Bay, August 5, 1864. Commended for coolness and close attention to duty in looking out for signals, and steering the ship in the action in Mobile Bay, on the morning and forenoon of August 5, 1864. He has been in the naval service eight years. Joined the "Brooklyn" in December, 1861; was in the actions with forts Jackson and St. Philip, and with the rebel iron-clads and gunboats below New Orleans; was in the action with the Chalmette batteries; present at the surrender of New Orleans, and in the attack on the batteries below Vicksburg, in 1862. Joined the "Richmond" in September, 1863.

Thomas Cripps,

Quartermaster on board of the United States steamer "Richmond," Mobile Bay, August 5, 1864. Commended for coolness and good conduct as captain of a gun in the action in Mobile Bay, on the morning and forenoon of August 5, 1864. He was in the "Brooklyn," in the actions with forts Jackson and St. Philip; the Chalmette batteries; batteries below Vicksburg; and present at the surrender of New Orleans. Joined the "Richmond" in September, 1863.

James B. Chandler,

Coxswain on board of the United States steamer "Richmond," Mobile Bay, August 5, 1864. Commended for coolness and good conduct in the action in Mobile Bay, on the morning and forenoon of August 5, 1864. He deserves especial notice for having come off the sick-list, and going to and remaining at his quarters during the entire action. Joined the "Brooklyn" in November, 1861; was in the actions with forts Jackson and St. Philip; the Chalmettes; batteries below Vicksburg; and present at the surrender of New Orleans. Joined the "Richmond" in September, 1863.

William W. Call,

Master at Arms on board of the United States steamer "Richmond," Mobile Bay, August 5, 1864. Commended for coolness, energy, and zeal in the action of Mobile Bay, on the morning and forenoon of August 5, 1864. Volunteered to direct, under the orders of the commander of the division, the passing of shells from the shell-rooms, in addition to his duties connected with the care of lights, which he performed most satisfactorily. Has been Master at Arms on board the "Richmond" since September, 1860; was in the actions with Fort McRea; at the head of the passes of the Mississippi; forts Jackson and St. Philip; the Chalmettes; the rebel iron-clads and gunboats below New Orleans; Vicksburg; Port Hudson; and present at the surrender of New Orleans.

WILLIAM DENSMORE,

Chief Boatswain's Mate on board of the United States steamer "Richmond," Mobile Bay, August 5, 1864. Commended for coolness and good conduct as captain of a gun in the action in Mobile Bay, on the morning and forenoon of August 5, 1864. He has been in the naval service twelve years; was on board the ship "St. Louis," blockading off Pensacola and the head of the passes of the Mississippi, until the expiration of his service in 1861; reshipped the same year, and joined the "Brooklyn"; was in the actions with forts Jackson and St. Philip, and with the rebel iron-clads and gunboats below New Orleans; was in the action with the Chalmette batteries; present at the surrender of New Orleans, and on board the "Brooklyn" in the attack upon the batteries below Vicksburg, in 1862. Joined the "Richmond" in September, 1863.

ADAM DUNCAN,

Boatswain's Mate on board of the United States steamer "Richmond," Mobile Bay, August 5, 1864. Commended for coolness and good conduct as captain of a gun in the action in Mobile Bay, on the morning and forenoon of

August 5, 1864. He has been six years in the naval service; was on board the "Brooklyn" in the actions with forts Jackson and St. Philip, and with the rebel iron-clads and gunboats below New Orleans; was in the action with the Chalmette batteries; present at the surrender of New Orleans, and on board the "Brooklyn" in the attack upon the batteries below Vicksburg, in 1862. Joined the "Richmond" in September, 1863.

CHARLES DEAKIN,

Boatswain's Mate on board of the United States steamer "Richmond," Mobile Bay, August 5, 1864. Commended for coolness and good conduct as captain of a gun in the action in Mobile Bay, on the morning and forenoon of August 5, 1864. He deserves special notice for his good example and zeal in going to and remaining at his quarters during the whole action, although quite sick. He has been in the naval service six years; was on board the "Brooklyn" in the actions with forts Jackson and St. Philip, and with the rebel iron-clads and gunboats below New Orleans; was in the action with the Chalmette batteries; present at the surrender of New Orleans, and on board the "Brooklyn" in the attack upon the batteries below Vicksburg, in 1862. Joined the "Richmond" in September, 1863.

WILLIAM DOOLIN,

Coal-heaver on board of the United States steamer "Richmond," Mobile Bay, August 5, 1864. Commended for coolness and good conduct, and for refusing to leave his station as shot and shell passer, after having been knocked down and badly wounded in the head by splinters; and upon going to quarters the second time, he was found at his station, nobly doing his duty in the action in Mobile Bay, on the morning and forenoon of August 5, 1864. He was in Fort Pickens when it was bombarded by the rebels; was on board the "Brooklyn" in the actions with forts Jackson and St. Philip; the Chalmettes; the rebel iron-clads and gunboats below New Orleans; the batteries below Vicksburg; and present at the surrender of New Orleans.

THOMAS HAYES,

Coxswain on board of the United States steamer "Richmond," Mobile Bay, August 5, 1864. Commended for coolness and good conduct as captain of No. 1 gun in the action in Mobile Bay, on the morning and forenoon of August 5, 1864. He was on board the "Brooklyn" in the actions with forts Jackson and St. Philip, and the iron-clads and gunboats below New Orleans; with the Chalmette batteries; batteries below Vicksburg; and was present at the surrender of New Orleans.

HUGH HAMILTON,

Coxswain on board of the United States steamer "Richmond," Mobile Bay, August 5, 1864. Commended for coolness and good conduct in the action in Mobile Bay, on the morning and forenoon of August 5, 1864. Was in the actions with forts Jackson and St. Philip; the Chalmettes; the rebel iron-clads and gunboats below New Orleans; the batteries below Vicksburg; present at the surrender of New Orleans. Joined the "Richmond" in October, 1863.

JAMES McINTOSH,

Captain of Top on board of the United States steamer "Richmond," Mobile Bay, August 5, 1864. Commended for coolness and good conduct in the action in Mobile Bay, on the morning and forenoon of August 5, 1864. He was present and assisted in the capture of the batteries at Hatteras Inlet, and on board the "Cumberland" when she was sunk by the "Merrimac," at Newport News. Joined the "Richmond" in September, 1863.

JOHN H. JAMES,

Captain of Top on board of the United States steamer "Richmond," Mobile Bay, August 5, 1864. Commended for coolness and good conduct as captain of a gun in the action in Mobile Bay, on the morning and forenoon of August 5, 1864. He came off the sick-list at the commencement of the action, went to his quarters, and fought his gun well during the entire action. He was in the actions with forts Jackson and St. Philip; the rebel ironclads and gunboats below New Orleans; the Chalmettes; the batteries below Vicksburg; and present at the surrender of New Orleans. Joined the "Richmond" September, 1863.

WILLIAM JONES,

Captain of Top on board of the United States steamer "Richmond," Mobile Bay, August 5, 1864. Commended for coolness and good conduct as captain of a gun in the action in Mobile Bay, on the morning and forenoon of the 5th of August, 1864. Joined the "Dacotah" in September, 1861, and was on board the "Cumberland" when sunk by the "Merrimac" at Newport News. Joined the "Richmond" in September, 1863.

JAMES H. MORGAN,

Captain of Top on board of the United States steamer "Richmond," Mobile Bay, August 5, 1864. Commended for coolness and good conduct as captain of a gun in the action in Mobile Bay, on the morning and forenoon of August 5, 1864. He joined the "Colorado" in May, 1861; volunteered for the United States steamer "Mississippi"; was in the action with forts Jackson and St. Philip; the Chalmettes; Vicksburg; Port Hudson; and present at the surrender of New Orleans; was on board the "New Ironsides," at Charleston. Joined the "Richmond" in October, 1863.

ANDREW MILLER,

Sergeant of Marines on board of the United States steamer "Richmond," Mobile Bay, August 5, 1864. Commended for coolness and good conduct as captain of a gun in the action in Mobile Bay, on the morning and forenoon of August 5, 1864. Was in the actions with forts Jackson and St. Philip; the Chalmettes; the rebel iron-clads and gunboats below New Orleans; batteries below Vicksburg; and present at the surrender of New Orleans.

JAMES MARTIN,

Sergeant of Marines on board of the United States steamer "Richmond," Mobile Bay, August 5, 1864. Commended for coolness and good conduct as captain of a gun in the action in Mobile Bay, on the morning and forenoon of August 5, 1864. Was in the actions with forts Jackson and St. Philip; the Chalmettes; the rebel iron-clads and gunboats below New Orleans; Vicksburg; Port Hudson; and present at the surrender of New Orleans, on board of the "Richmond."

GEORGE PARKS,

Captain of Forecastle on board of the United States steamer "Richmond," Mobile Bay, August 5, 1864. Commended for coolness and good conduct in the action in Mobile Bay, on the morning and forenoon of August 5, 1864. He joined the "Richmond" in September, 1860; reshipped, October, 1863; was in the actions with Fort McRea; with the rebel vessels at the head of the passes of the Mississippi; in passing forts Jackson and St. Philip; the Chalmettes; twice before Vicksburg batteries; at Port Hudson; was captain of a gun in the naval nine-inch gun battery at the siege of Port Hudson, and present at the surrender of New Orleans.

HENDRICK SHARP,

Seaman on board of the United States steamer "Richmond," Mobile Bay, August 5, 1864. Commended for coolness and courage as captain of one hundred-pounder rifle gun on topgallant forecastle in the action in Mobile Bay, on the morning and forenoon of August 5, 1864. He fought his gun when under the hottest fire from the enemy's batteries, at short range, with a coolness and effectiveness that won not only the admiration of the commanding officer of the division, but of all others who had an opportunity to observe him. He has been in the naval service thirty-two years; joined the "Richmond" at Norfolk when first put in commission, September 27,

1860. At the expiration of his term of service, in 1863, reshipped for the period of three years. He was in action on board of the "Richmond" with the rebels at the head of the passes of the Mississippi; at the bombardment of Fort McRea, at Pensacola, which lasted an entire day, when he received a severe splinter wound in the left hand which permanently disabled two of his fingers; and notwithstanding the severity of the wound, as soon as it was dressed by the surgeon he returned to his gun without the permission of the surgeon, and persisted in remaining at his quarters, using his right hand until the action ceased. He was in the actions with forts Jackson and St. Philip, and with the rebel iron-clads and gunboats below New Orleans; in action with the Chalmette batteries; present at the surrender of New Orleans; fought the batteries of Vicksburg twice; was in the memorable attack on Port Hudson, on the 14th of March, 1863; was captain of a nine-inch gun in the naval nine-inch gun battery, commanded by Lieutenant-Commander Edward Terry, placed in the rear of Port Hudson during the siege. He was also captain of a gun in the naval battery established at Baton Rouge, and commanded by Lieutenant-Commander Edward Terry, after the repulse of the army and death of General Williams at that place.

WALTER B. SMITH,

Ordinary Seaman on board of the United States steamer "Richmond," Mobile Bay, August 5, 1864. Commended for coolness and good conduct at the one hundred-pounder rifle gun on the topgallant forecastle, and for musket-firing into the gunports of the rebel iron-clad "Tennessee," in the action in Mobile Bay, on the morning and forenoon of August 5, 1864. He was on board the United States steamer "Hatteras" when that vessel was sunk by the Alabama, commanded by Captain Semmes, off Galveston; joined the "Richmond" after having been exchanged, September, 1863; and his good conduct on board of that ship has been of the most exemplary kind.

LEBBEUS SIMPKINS,

Coxswain on board of the United States steamer "Richmond," Mobile Bay, August 5, 1864. Commended for coolness and courage in the action in Mobile Bay, on the morning and forenoon of August 5, 1864. He joined the "Brooklyn" in January, 1861; was in the actions with forts Jackson and St. Philip, and the rebel iron-clads and gunboats below New Orleans; Chalmette batteries; batteries below Vicksburg; and present at the surrender of New Orleans. Joined the "Richmond," October, 1863.

OLOFF SMITH,

Coxswain on board of the United States steamer "Richmond," Mobile Bay, August 5, 1864. Commended for coolness and good conduct in the action in Mobile Bay, on the morning and forenoon of August 5, 1864. He was on board the "Richmond" in the actions with Fort McRea; at the head of the passes of the Mississippi; with forts Jackson and St. Philip; the rebel iron-clads and gunboats below New Orleans; the Chalmette batteries; twice with the batteries of Vicksburg in attempting to pass; and at the siege of Port Hudson; and present at the surrender of New Orleans. He has been coxswain on board the "Richmond" for twenty consecutive months.

JOHN SMITH,

Second Captain of Top on board of the United States steamer "Richmond," Mobile Bay, August 5, 1864. Commended for coolness and good conduct as captain of a gun in the action in Mobile Bay, on the morning and forenoon of August 5, 1864. He was on board the "Varuna" when she was sunk by the rebel vessels after having passed forts Jackson and St. Philip; was transferred to the "Brooklyn"; and was in the action with the batteries below Vicksburg. Joined the "Richmond" in September, 1863.

JAMES SMITH,

Captain of Forecastle on board the United States steamer "Richmond," Mobile Bay, August 5, 1864. Commended for coolness and good conduct as captain of a gun in the action in Mobile Bay, on the morning and forenoon of August 5, 1864.

DAVID SPROWLE,

Orderly Sergeant of the Marine Guard on board of the United States steamer "Richmond," Mobile Bay, August 5, 1864. Commended for coolness, and for setting a good example to the marine guard working a division of great guns in the action of Mobile Bay, on the morning and forenoon of August 5, 1864. Joined the "Richmond," September 27, 1860; was in the actions with Fort McRea; the head of the passes of the Mississippi; forts Jackson and St. Philip; the Chalmettes; the rebel iron-clads and gunboats below New Orleans; Vicksburg; Port Hudson; and present at the surrender of New Orleans. He has been in the service twenty-eight years.

Alexander H. Truett,

Coxswain on board of the United States steamer "Richmond," Mobile Bay, August 5, 1864. Commended for coolness and good conduct in the action in Mobile Bay, on the morning and forenoon of August 5, 1864. He was in the actions with forts Jackson and St. Philip; the Chalmette batteries; the rebel iron-clads and gunboats below New Orleans; the batteries below Vicksburg; and was present at the surrender of New Orleans. He was present at and assisted in the capture of the piratical steamers "Maramon" and "Marquis de la Habana," in March, 1860, near Vera Cruz.

John M. Burns,

Seaman on board of the United States steamer "Lackawanna." Severely wounded and sent below under the surgeon's charge; would not remain unemployed, but assisted the powder division until the action was over.

Michael Cassidy,

Landsman on board of the United States steamer "Lackawanna." First sponger of a gun. Displayed great coolness and exemplary behavior, eliciting the applause of his officers and the gun's crew.

Louis G. Chaput,

Landsman on board of the United States steamer "Lackawanna." Remained at his gun after he was severely wounded until relieved by another person; was then taken below, and after reporting to the surgeon returned to his station at the gun, and resumed his duties until the action was over, and was then carried below.

Adam McCullock,

Seaman on board of the United States steamer "Lackawanna." Being wounded, would not leave his quarters, although ordered to do so, but remained until the action was over.

Patrick Dougherty,

Landsman on board of the United States steamer "Lackawanna." Took the place of the powder-boy at his gun without orders, when the powder-boy was disabled; kept up a supply, and showed much zeal in his new capacity.

John Edwards,

Captain of Top on board of the United States steamer "Lackawanna." Second captain of a gun. Although wounded, would not, when ordered, go below to the surgeon, but took the place of the first captain during the remainder of the action.

Samuel W. Kinnaird,

Landsman on board of the United States steamer "Lackawanna." Set an example to the crew by his presence of mind and cheerfulness, that had a beneficial effect.

WILLIAM PHINNEY,

Boatswain's Mate on board of the United States steamer "Lackawanna." As captain of a gun, showed much presence of mind and coolness in managing it, and gave great encouragement to the crew.

JOHN SMITH,

Captain of Forecastle on board of the United States steamer "Lackawanna." Was first captain of a gun, and finding that he could not sufficiently depress his gun, when alongside of the rebel iron-clad "Tennessee," threw a hand holy-stone into one of the ports at a rebel using abusive language against the crew of the ship.

GEORGE TAYLOR,

Armorer on board of the United States steamer "Lackawanna"; although wounded, went into the shell-room, and with his hands extinguished the fire from a shell exploded over it by the enemy.

JAMES WARD,

Quarter Gunner on board of the United States steamer "Lackawanna." Being wounded, and ordered below, would not go, but rendered much aid at one of the guns when the crew was disabled, and subsequently remained in the chains heaving the lead until nearly in collision with the rebel iron-clad "Tennessee."

Daniel Whitfield,

Quartermaster on board of the United States steamer "Lackawanna." Remarkable coolness as captain of a gun in holding on to the lock-string and waiting for some time whilst alongside of the rebel iron-clad "Tennessee," and firing so that the shot might enter her port.

William Gardner,

Seaman on board of the United States steamer "Oneida." Behaved so coolly under fire as to draw the particular attention of the executive officer of the vessel.

John E. Jones,

Quartermaster on board of the United States steamer "Oneida." Stationed at the wheel; was wounded. After the wheel-ropes were shot away, he went on the poop to assist at the signals, and remained there until ordered to reeve new wheel-ropes.

Thomas Kendrick,

Coxswain on board of the United States steamer "Oneida." A volunteer from the "Bienville." Attracted the particular attention of the executive officer of the "Oneida" by his excellent conduct.

William Newland,

Ordinary Seaman on board of the United States steamer "Oneida." First loader of the after nine-inch gun. Mentioned as having behaved splendidly, and as being distinguished on board for good conduct and faithful discharge of all duties.

DAVID NAYLOR,

Landsman on board of the United States steamer "Oneida." Powder-boy at the thirty-pounder Parrott rifle. His passing-box having been knocked out of his hand, fell overboard into a boat alongside. He immediately jumped overboard, recovered it, and returned to his station.

JOHN PRESTON,

Landsman on board of the United States steamer "Oneida." Although severely wounded, he remained at his gun until obliged to go to the surgeon, to whom he reported himself as slightly hurt. He assisted in taking care of the wounded below, and wanted to return to his station, but on examining him it was found that he was wounded quite severely in both eyes.

JAMES S. ROANTREE,

Sergeant of Marines on board of the United States steamer "Oneida." Conducted himself with distinguished gallantry, and is mentioned as particularly deserving of notice.

JAMES SHERIDAN,

Quartermaster on board of the United States steamer "Oneida." Captain of the after nine-inch gun; was wounded in several places, but remained at his gun until the firing ceased, and then supplied the place of the Signal Quartermaster, who had been injured by a fall.

Charles B. Woram,

Seaman on board of the United States steamer "Oneida." Acting as aid to the executive officer. Distinguished himself for his cool courage, and carried his orders intelligently and correctly.

Andrew Jones,

Chief Boatswain's Mate on board of the United States steamer "Chickasaw." Although his enlistment had expired, he volunteered from the "Vincennes" for the battles in Mobile Bay, and was honorably mentioned by the commanding officer of the "Chickasaw."

EXTRACTS FROM LETTERS SENT FROM HEAD-QUARTERS MILITARY DIVISION WEST MISSISSIPPI.

HEAD-QUARTERS MILITARY DIVISION OF THE WEST MISSISSIPPI,
NEW ORLEANS, LA., August 9, 1864.

MAJOR-GENERAL H. W. HALLECK,
Chief of Staff, Washington, D. C.

SIR: Fort Gaines, with forty-six commissioned officers, and eight hundred and eighteen enlisted men, with its armament, twenty-six guns, intact, and provisions for twelve months, has surrendered (unconditionally). It was occupied by our own forces at eight o'clock, yesterday morning.

Fort Powell was abandoned, its garrison escaping to Cedar Point. Its armament, eighteen guns, is in condition for immediate service.

General Granger, reinforced by two thousand men, will immediately invest Fort Morgan, leaving garrisons in forts Gaines and Powell.

E. R. S. CANBY,
Major-General, commanding.

HEAD-QUARTERS MILITARY DIVISION OF THE WEST MISSISSIPPI,
    NEW ORLEANS, LA., August 24, 1864.

MAJOR-GENERAL H. W. HALLECK,
    Chief of Staff, Washington, D. C.

SIR: By the surrender of Fort Morgan we have about six hundred prisoners, sixty pieces of artillery, and a large quantity of material. In the twelve hours preceding the surrender, about three thousand shells were thrown into the fort. The citadel and barracks are entirely destroyed, the works generally much injured. Many of the guns were spiked, the carriages burned, and much of the ammunition destroyed by the rebels.

The losses in the army were one man killed and seven wounded.

                    E. R. S. CANBY,
                            Major-General, commanding.

B. B. K.
  H. E.

EXTRACTS FROM CONFEDERATE OFFICIAL REPORTS.

Mobile, August 7, 1864.

Colonel: I have the honor to report the evacuation and destruction of Fort Powell, on the night of August 5th.

When the enemy's fleet passed into the bay, the garrison consisted of two (2) companies of the Twenty-first Alabama Regiment, and part of Culpepper's Battery, — in all about one hundred and forty men. Water for thirty days was protected from the enemy's fire in the bomb-proof, and other stores for two months. The front face of the work was nearly completed and in a defensible condition, mounting one eight-inch columbiad, one six and four-tenths-inch rifle, and two seven-inch Brooks guns. The face looking towards Gaines and Little Dauphine Island was half finished. The parapet was nearly complete, but traverses and galleries had only been framed. The rear had only been commenced. Two guns were mounted, — one ten-inch columbiad, and one seven-inch Brooks rifled. They were without parapets, and exposed from the platform up. This part of the fort was strewed with a large quantity of lumber, which was being used in the construction of galleries, magazines, &c. During the morning, the fort was shelled from five gunboats in the sound, at long range. The fort was hit five times, but no particular damage was done.

APPENDIX. 121

I replied with the four guns bearing on that side, with what effect is not known. About 2.30 P. M., one of the enemy's monitors came up within seven hundred yards of the fort, firing rapidly with shell and grape. I replied from the seven-inch Brooks gun (razeed) on the southern angle. It was protected by an unfinished traverse, which however would not permit it to be depressed sufficiently for ricochet firing. The gun was loaded with great difficulty, there being no platform for the gunners in the rear, owing to which, and the delay occasioned by a sponge-head pulling off in the gun, I succeeded in firing but three shots from it while the iron-clad was in range. One shot struck on the bow, with no apparent effect. The iron-clad's fire made it impossible to man the two guns in the rear, and I made no attempt to do so.

The elevating machine of the ten-inch columbiad was broken by a fragment of shell. A shell entered one of the sally-ports, which are not traversed in the rear, passed entirely through the bomb-proof, and buried itself in the opposite wall; fortunately it did not explode. The shells exploding in the face of the work displaced the sand so rapidly, that I was convinced, that unless the iron-clad was driven off, it would explode my magazine and make the bomb-proof chambers untenable, in two days at the furthest. To drive it from its position I believed impossible with my imperfect work, and so telegraphed to Colonel Anderson, commanding Fort Gaines, that unless I could evacuate I would be compelled to surrender within forty-eight hours. His reply was, "Save your garrison when your fort is no longer tenable."

At the time his despatch was received it was becoming dark. The fleet had not moved up to intercept my communication with Cedar Point; I could not expect to have another opportunity for escape, and I decided promptly that it would be better to save my command and destroy the fort, than to allow both to fall into the hands of the enemy, as they certainly would have done in two days. The tide being low, I marched my command to Cedar Point without interruption or discovery. In one narrow channel I found the water overhead, and in crossing it I damaged my ammunition and lost a few muskets (a special report of which will be made).

Lieutenant Savage was left in the fort, with orders to prepare a train and match, to explode the magazine as soon as he discovered that I had gained the mainland. Lieutenant Jeffers, Acting Ordnance Officer, was directed to spike the guns at the same time. The fort was blown up at 10.30 P. M. Every man was brought off safely to Cedar Point, thence to the city.

Respectfully, your obedient servant,
J. M. WILLIAMS,
Lieutenant-Colonel, commanding.

COL. G. G. GARNER, *Chief of Staff.*

HEAD-QUARTERS DISTRICT OF THE GULF,
MOBILE, ALABAMA, August 9, 1864.

GENERAL: While at Meridian on the 3d instant, I received despatches indicating a land and naval attack on the lower forts. On the 4th instant, a force was thrown on Dauphine Island estimated at two thousand (2000). On Friday, the 5th instant, the enemy's fleet attacked Fort Morgan, at 6.30 A. M. After several hours' bombardment, the whole fleet, except one large monitor, which was sunk by our guns, ran by the fort and entered the bay. They numbered (14) fourteen wooden ships, and (3) three iron-clads. The Tennessee, and little gunboats Selma, Gaines, and Morgan, were soon overpowered. The conduct of the Admiral, in the Tennessee, and of the Selma, Captain Pat. Murphy, is spoken of as devotedly gallant.

On the same day a monitor ran close up to Fort Powell and cannonaded it for several hours; (5) five gunboats in Mississippi Sound bombarded it at long range. No serious injury was done to the fort, besides disabling the carriage of a ten-inch gun. No officer or man was wounded. That night, Lieutenant-Colonel Williams, the same commander who, in a spirited manner, sustained the attack of Farragut some months ago, evacuated the fort, blew it up, and brought the garrison to this city. Urgent orders were sent to Colonel C. D. Anderson, Twenty-first Alabama, the commander of Gaines, to hold his fort to the last extremity.

He surrendered his fort with about six hundred (600) good troops in it, on yesterday morning.

The commander and garrison of Fort Morgan evince a noble spirit of resolution.

Grant's Pass is now open for transports, and Mobile may be attacked in a short time. Henceforth the place must always be held ready for attack. There are an unusual number of women and children here; they will not go away until the shells begin to fall, when it may be too late. There is six months' supply of victuals here for a garrison. The ordnance supplies are still insufficient for siege. The citizens, employés, reserves, militia, (2) two Louisiana regiments of heavy artillery, (6) six companies of cavalry, and a battalion of men selected from companies of correction, in all about (4,000), four thousand, now man the works.

A regiment of reserves, and about (300) three hundred artillerists are *en route*. Other reserves are under orders to come here — (say 1,000). Last night I received a despatch from my most intelligent New Orleans correspondent, stating Canby's force at 3,000. If this be so, no immediate attack upon the city is probable. Forrest telegraphs me that the force advancing down the Mississippi Central road is about 15,000 men. It has forced Chalmers back towards Oxford. Forrest has about (7,000) seven thousand veteran cavalry. I have ordered General Wirt Adams and Liddell to reinforce him, if possible. They may send him 1,000 to 1,500 men, and the State reserves and militia of Mississippi may give him 1,500 more. With this I think he can retard, and perhaps defeat the enemy. I go to Meridian this evening. No tidings yet of General Taylor, or of troops crossing.

Very respectfully, your obedient servant,

DABNEY H. MAURY,
Major-General, commanding.

APPENDIX. 125

HEAD-QUARTERS DEPARTMENT OF ALABAMA, MISSISSIPPI,
AND EASTERN LOUISIANA,
MOBILE, ALA., August 12, 1864.

MY DEAR SIR: I received to-day your despatch inquiring for the particulars concerning the surrender of Fort Gaines. I have answered as to the main points. When the fleet first appeared to be increasing before Fort Morgan, I was in Meridian, the head-quarters of the department to which I had recently been temporarily assigned. On my return to Mobile, on the 3d instant, I found that, in consequence of the appearance of a land force off Dauphine Island, the garrisons of forts Gaines and Powell had been increased by sending some local troops (Pelham Cadets), marines, reserves, heavy artillery — in fact, almost every available soldier at that time in Mobile. It was then believed those would hold out against any attack likely to be made on them, and it was hoped the fleet would not enter the bay.

Lieutenant-Colonel Williams, of Fort Powell, abandoned and blew up his work without having a man injured, nor had any injury been inflicted on any part of his fort. He reports one of his gun-carriages disabled, and one gun temporarily out of use by careless loading. He had under his bomb-proof fully thirty (30) days' water, and two months' provisions. He had hand-grenades, revolvers, muskets, and howitzers to defend his fort against launches, and eight (8) heavy guns to use against the ships. The fort had just been connected, by telegraph, with Fort Gaines and with Mobile. On the morning of the 5th, there were seventy (70) negroes, with trenching tools, in the fort; the guns on the east face of the work were mounted and in fighting order, but were not yet covered by the parapet, and the men serving them would have been exposed, as are sailors on an ordinary man-of-war.

It is altogether probable that a faithful service of their battery for half an hour would have driven off or sunk the only boat attacking its eastern face, and that it might have been held long enough to compel the fleet to put to sea, or at least to enable Mobile to prepare fully for land attack.

Fort Gaines was garrisoned by six (6) companies Twenty-first Alabama regiment, two (2) companies First Alabama battalion, forty (40) Pelham Cadets, one hundred and twenty (120) reserves, and about forty (40) marines — in all about (600) six hundred good troops. The fort was well supplied for (6) six months. The three (3) ten-inch guns were dismounted* during the bombardment; twenty (20) guns remained in good order. The fort was uninjured, and could have long withstood attack. The enclosed copy of General Page's despatch reveals all I know of the surrender.

The important consequence of these misfortunes is, that Mobile is henceforth liable to attack without warning, and must always be ready for siege. I have heretofore, as you know, sent from here troops and supplies to other points, which seemed more important or more imminently pressed; henceforth I must collect and hold here everything necessary for a beleaguered city.

The heavy armament calls for a great deal of ammunition. The outer line — Morgan, Gaines, and Powell —

---

* Temporarily dismounted during the bombardment by the carelessness of the cannoneers; afterwards remounted, according to information just received.

was supplied with three hundred (300) rounds per gun. The guns near the city have not more than two hundred (200). The total number of men now under arms in the whole district is about (6,000) six thousand — about (1,000) one thousand of whom have been under fire, and a large portion are citizens of the place.

The city has probably more women and children in it than at any time since the war began.

I am, sir, very respectfully,
Your obedient servant,
DABNEY H. MAURY,
Major-General, commanding.

HON. JAMES A. SEDDON, *Secretary of War, C. S. N., Richmond, Va.*

HEAD-QUARTERS DEPARTMENT OF ALABAMA,
MISSISSIPPI, AND EAST LOUISIANA,
MOBILE, ALA., September 1, 1864.

GENERAL SAMUEL COOPER,
Adjutant and Inspector-General, C. S. A., Richmond, Va.

GENERAL: When I was assigned to the command of this department, July 26th, it had been stripped of most of its troops to strengthen the Army of Tennessee. In Mobile, there was not a soldier, except the artillery garrisons of the forts and bay batteries. Forrest, with six thousand effective cavalry, guarded North Mississippi against a heavy column advancing from Memphis. General Wirt Adams, with five or six hundred cavalry, watched Vicksburg; Colonel Scott, with twelve hundred cavalry, held East Louisiana. A few disorganized fragments of brigades, numbering a thousand men, perhaps, with some companies of state reserves, constituted my force in North and Central Alabama.

The enemy prepared to move on Mobile and North Mississippi simultaneously.

On the 5th of August, a very formidable fleet of iron-clad and wooden ships, led by Admiral Farragut, after a fierce bombardment of Fort Morgan, ran past that fortress, and entered Mobile Bay. One iron-clad, the Tecumseh, was sunk by a torpedo,* and a small gunboat, the Philippi, was destroyed by our fire. On the same day, a monitor ran up within seven hundred yards of Fort Powell, and bombarded it for several hours. The garrison suffered no loss; the fort sustained no serious damage. That night, the commander evacuated and blew up the fort, thus leaving Grant's Pass open to the enemy. He is now undergoing trial before a court-martial.

On the evening of August 3d, the enemy had landed a force on Dauphine Island, in order to besiege and reduce Fort Gaines. General Page called for reinforcements, to enable him to attack this force, which at that time he supposed to be small. Every available man was sent from Mobile to Fort Gaines. The entrance of the fleet into the bay prevented their return to the city. They were too few to make the proposed attack, but were too many for the proper siege garrison of Fort Gaines, and for the unexplained precipitate surrender made by Colonel Anderson of a work which, faithfully defended, could have held the enemy before it at least as long as Fort Morgan.

---

* General Page reports that it was sunk by the guns of Fort Morgan.

After firing a few shots, Colonel Anderson, without authority, entered into negotiations with the enemy, and on the 7th instant, the Confederate flag was lowered, and the ensign of the enemy raised and saluted. General Page reports that he visited Fort Gaines, and used every proper means to prevent its surrender. He could not with propriety assume command at Fort Gaines, and remain absent from his more important command at Fort Morgan. He ordered Colonel Anderson to be relieved from command, and forbade any surrender unless the Federals should return with Colonel Anderson to the fort. Nothing more is known of this unfortunate affair. It enabled the enemy at once to concentrate all his efforts upon Fort Morgan, which was invested and besieged. In the course of a few days all communication was cut off with that fortress, and we could only infer anything of its fate from the distant sound of the cannon, and the uncertain reports of our scouts along the bay shore.

After sustaining a very heavy attack by the army and the fleet, General Page surrendered his fort and garrison on the 23d instant. From the statements of the enemy, we learn that their batteries had crowned the glacis. The citadel had repeatedly been set on fire, and the flag of the fort was not lowered until the work was no longer tenable. General Page is also reported to have destroyed everything in the fort which could be of service to the enemy before surrendering.

I am, General, very respectfully,
    Your obedient servant,
        DABNEY H. MAURY,
          Major-General, commanding.

FORT MORGAN, 12 M., August 23, 1864.

MAJOR-GENERAL D. H. MAURY,
  or Commanding Officer, District Mobile.

GENERAL: I held the fort as long as it was tenable; the parallels of the enemy had reached the glacis; the walls were breached; all the guns save two were disabled; the wood-work of the citadel, being repeatedly fired by the shells of the enemy, endangered the magazines. All my powder was destroyed, every gun effectually spiked, and otherwise damaged, and indeed the whole fort (everything that could prove of value to the enemy) is now a mass of *debris.*

I turn this over to their forces at two o'clock to-day. The garrison behaved gallantly, and gained honor for themselves and country.

    Respectfully, &c.,
      R. L. PAGE, *Brigadier-General.*

OFFICE TORPEDO BUREAU, RICHMOND, August 15, 1864.

HON. JAMES A. SEDDON, *Secretary of War, C. S.*

SIR: I have the honor to enclose the within telegram, with the remark that, previous to leaving Mobile, I had sixty-seven (67) torpedoes planted where this one acted, and had nine (9) sub-marine mortar batteries under way (three completed) to close the main channel, such as the enemy report kept them out of Charleston; they being unable to remove them.

But my instructions and wishes were frustrated after I left; the place left open, and the enemy made use of it.

>Very respectfully,
>>Your obedient servant,
>>>G. J. RAINS,
>>>>*Brigadier-General, superintendent.*

TELEGRAM.

Received at Richmond, August 13, 1864, at — o'clock, — minutes:

By telegraph, from Mobile, 13, to General G. J. Rains.

Monitor Tecumseh was sunk by torpedo in thirty seconds.

>>>F. S. BARRETT.

$\frac{9|880}{G.}$

[INDORSEMENT.]

From Lieutenant Barrett, in charge of torpedo defences at Mobile, Alabama.

ARMAMENT AND WEIGHT OF PROJECTILES OF UNION VESSELS ENGAGED IN THE BATTLE OF MOBILE BAY.

NAME.	GUNS.	Solid Shot. lbs.	Cored Shot. lbs.	Shell. lbs.	Shrapnel. lbs.	Grape. lbs.	Canister. lbs.
Brooklyn.....	2 100-Pdr. Parrotts.	70		80	86		
	2 60-Pdr. Parrotts.	60		50			
	20 IX-inch Guns.	90	73	72½	75	74	70
	Total Weight.	2060	1460	1710	1672	1480	1400
Octorora......	1 100-Pdr. Parrott.	70		80	86		
	2 32-Pdr. 33 *Cut.*	32		26	32	33½	30
	3 IX-inch.	90	73	72½	75	74	70
	4 24-Pdrs.			20	26		
	Total Weight.	404	219	429	479	289	270
Hartford	2 100-Pdr. Parrotts.	70		80	86		
	1 30-Pdr. Parrott.	30		29			
	18 IX-inch.	90	73	72½	75	74	70
	Total Weight.	1790	1314	1494	1522	1332	1260
Metacomet....	2 100-Pdr. Parrotts.	70		80			
	4 IX-inch.	90	73	72½	75	74	70
	2 24-Pdrs.			20	26		17
	2 12-Pdrs.			10	13		11
	Total Weight,	500	292	510	378	296	336
Richmond	1 100-Pdr. Parrott.	70		80			
	1 30-Pdr. Parrott.	30		29			
	18 IX-inch.	90	73	72½	75	74	70
	Total Weight.	1720	1314	1414	1350	1332	1260
Port Royal...	1 100-Pdr. Parrott.	70		80	86		
	1 X-inch.	124		103	101		69
	2 50-Pdrs.	50		50			
	2 IX-inch.	90	73	72½	75	74	70
	2 24-Pdrs.			20	26		
	Total Weight.	474	146	468	389	148	209

NAME.	Guns.	Solid Shot. lbs.	Cored Shot. lbs.	Shell. lbs.	Shrapnel. lbs.	Grape. lbs.	Canister. lbs.
Lackawanna..	1 150-Pdr. Parrott.	135		135			
	1 50-Pdr.	50		50			
	2 XI-inch.	166		136	141	125	150
	4 IX-inch.	90	73	72½	75	74	70
	2 24-Pdrs.			20	26		17
	4 12-Pdrs.			12			11
	Total Weight.	877	292	835	634	546	658
Seminole	1 30-Pdr. Parrott.	30		29			
	6 32-Pdrs.	32		26	32	33½	30
	1 XI-inch.	166		136	141	125	150
	Total Weight.	388		321	333	326	330
Monongahela .	1 150-Pdr. Parrott.	135		135			
	2 XI-inch.	166		136	141	125	150
	5 32-Pdrs. 57 *Cut*.	32		26	32	33½	30
	2 24-Pdrs.			20	26		17
	1 12-Pdr.			12			11
	Total Weight.	627		589	494	417	495
Kennebec	1 20-Pdr. Parrott.			19	20		
	1 XI-inch.	166		136	141	125	150
	2 24-Pdrs.			20	26	24	17
	1 12-Pdr.			12	12		11
	Total Weight,	166		207	225	173	195
Ossipee.......	1 100-Pdr. Parrott.	70		80			
	1 XI-inch.	166		136	141	125	150
	6 32-Pdrs. 42 *Cut*.	32		26	32	33	30
	3 30-Pdr. Parrotts.	30		29			
	2 12-Pdrs.	12		12	12+		10½+
	Total Weight.	542		483	357+	323	351+
Itaska........	1 XI-inch.	166		136	141	125	
	2 20-Pdr. Parrotts.			19	20		
	2 32-Pdrs. 57 *Cut*.	32		26	32	33½	30
	1 12-Pdr.			12			11
	Total Weight.	230		238	245	192	71

NAME.	Guns.	Solid Shot. lbs.	Cored Shot. lbs.	Shell. lbs.	Shrapnel. lbs.	Grape. lbs.	Canister. lbs.
Oneida	2 XI-inch.	166		136	141	125	150
	3 30-Pdr. Parrotts.	30		29			
	4 32-Pdrs. 33 *Cut*.	32		26	32	33½	30
	1 12-Pdr.			12			11
	Total Weight.	550		475	410	384	431
Galena	1 100-Pdr. Parrott.	70		80	86		
	1 30-Pdr. Parrott.	30		29			
	8 IX-inch.	90	73	72½	75	74	70
	1 12-Pdr.			12			11
	Total Weight.	820	584	701	686	592	571
Tecumseh	2 XV-inch.	440	400	350	358	332	197
	Total Weight.	880	800	700	716	664	394
Manhattan	2 XV-inch.	440	400	350	358	332	197
	Total Weight,	880	800	700	716	664	394
Winnebago	4 XI-inch.	166		136	141	125	150
	Total Weight.	664		544	564	500	600
Chickasaw	4 XI-inch.	166		136	141	125	150
	Total Weight.	664		544	564	500	600

The armament of Farragut's fleet in 1864 was considered, both in Europe and America, exceedingly formidable. How guns have increased in size since then the following extract from Chief Engineer King's valuable "Report on European Ships of War" will show. By it the reader will see that the "Intrepid" throws at a broadside rather more than two-thirds of the weight of metal thrown by our eighteen vessels.

APPENDIX. 135

"The armament of the *Inflexible* will be composed of four of the heaviest guns (except those making for the Italian vessels) ever constructed, of which the experimental eighty-one ton gun completed at Woolwich, and tested, is the type. They are capable of being fired, all four together, at an enemy ahead, astern, or abeam, and, in pairs, toward every point of the compass.

"The gun is rifled with thirteen grooves, each having an increasing pitch from 0 to 1 in thirty-five calibres. The

Number of Rounds.	Size of Powder.	Weight of Charge.	Weight of Projectile.	Muzzle Velocity per Second.	Mean Pressure in Gun.	Total Energy developed.
	Cubic Inches.	Pounds.	Pounds.	Feet.	Tons per Sq. Inch.	Foot-tons.
1	1.5	340	1,700	1,486	20.1	26,030
2	1.5	350	1,700	1,505	20.4	26,740
3	1.5	350	1,700	1,502	20.3	26,630
4	1.5	350	1,700	1,467	19.6	25,406
5	1.5	350	1,700	1,475	18.4	25,683
6	1.5	350	1,700	1,493	21.0	26,314
7	1.5	360	1,700	1,487	18.8	26,103
8	1.5	370	1,700	1,495	19.9	26,385
9	1.5	350	1,700	1,518	20.5	27,203
10	1.5	370	1,700	1,523	20.3	27,383
11	1.5	360	1,700	1,519	21.3	27,239
12	1.5	360	1,700	1,518	20.0	27,203
13	1.5	370	1,700	1,519	19.8	27,239
14	1.5	370	1,700	1,517	20.7	27,168

service powder-charge is three hundred and seventy pounds of 1.5 inch powder. The weight of the projectile for the service-shell is one thousand seven hundred pounds, and the bursting charge about one hundred pounds of powder. The details of the series of proof-trials at Woolwich, also the tests at Shoeburyness, have been widely published. Still, for reference, it is believed advisable to give (p. 135) the results of the trials last made with the calibre of sixteen inches — that at which the gun is to be used in actual warfare."

www.ingramcontent.com/pod-product-compliance
Lightning Source LLC
Chambersburg PA
CBHW022134160426
43197CB00009B/1285